Japanese Distribution Channels

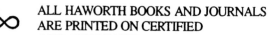

Japanese Distribution Channels

Takeshi Kikuchi
Editor

The Haworth Press, Inc.
New York • London • Norwood (Australia)

Japanese Distribution Channels has also been published as *Journal of Marketing Channels*, Volume 3, Number 3 1994.

The development, preparation, and publication of this work has been undertaken with great care. However, the publisher, employees, editors, and agents of The Haworth Press and all imprints of The Haworth Press, Inc., including The Haworth Medical Press and Pharmaceutical Products Press, are not responsible for any errors contained herein or for consequences that may ensue from use of materials or information contained in this work. Opinions expressed by the author(s) are not necessarily those of The Haworth Press, Inc.

The Haworth Press, Inc., 10 Alice Street, Binghamton, NY 13904-1580 USA

Library of Congress Cataloging-in-Publication Data

Japanese distribution channels / Takeshi Kikuchi, editor.
    p. cm.
    "Japanese distribution channels has also been published as Journal of marketing channels, v. 3. no. 3 1994"–CIP pub. info.
    Includes bibliographical references.
    ISBN 1-56024-702-9 (acid-free paper)
    1. Marketing channels–Japan. 2. Physical distribution of goods–Japan. I. Kikuchi, Takeshi, 1931- .
HF5415.129.J36 1994   94-34089
381'.0952–dc20   CIP

INDEXING & ABSTRACTING

Contributions to this publication are selectively indexed or abstracted in print, electronic, online, or CD-ROM version(s) of the reference tools and information services listed below. This list is current as of the copyright date of this publication. See the end of this section for additional notes.

- *ABSCAN, Inc.*, P.O. Box 2384, Monroe, LA 71207-2384

- *Contents Pages in Management*, University of Manchester Business School, Booth Street West, Manchester M15 6PB, England

- *Engineering Information (PAGE ONE)*, Bibliographic Services Department, Castle Point on the Hudson, Hoboken, NJ 07030

- *Food Science and Technology Abstracts (FSTA) Scanned, abstracted and indexed by the International Food Information Service (IFIS) for inclusion in Food Science and Technology Abstracts (FSTA),* International Food Information Service, Lane End House, Shinfield, Reading RG2 9BB, England

- *Foods Adlibra*, Foods Adlibra Publications, 9000 Plymouth Avenue North, Minneapolis, MN 55427

- *Human Resources Abstracts (HRA)*, Sage Publications, Inc., 2455 Teller Road, Newbury Park, CA 91320

(continued)

- *INSPEC Information Services,* Institution of Electrical Engineers, Michael Faraday House, Six Hills Way, Stevenage, Herts SG1 2AY, England

- *Management & Marketing Abstracts,* Pira International, Randalls Road, Leatherhead, Surrey KT22 7RU, England

- *Operations Research/Management Science,* Executive Sciences Institute, 1005 Mississippi Avenue, Davenport, IA 52803

- *Referativnyi Zhurnal (Abstracts Journal of the Institute of Scientific Information of the Republic of Russia),* The Institute of Scientific Information, Baltijskaja ul., 14, Moscow A-219, Republic of Russia

- *Social Planning/Policy & Development Abstracts (SOPODA),* Sociological Abstracts, Inc., P.O. Box 22206, San Diego, CA 92192-0206

- *Sociological Abstracts (SA),* Sociological Abstracts, Inc., P.O. Box 22206, San Diego, CA 92192-0206

- *World Agricultural Economics & Rural Sociology Abstracts (CAB Abstracts),* c/o CAB International ACCESS . . . available in print, diskettes updated weekly, and on INTERNET. Providing full bibliographic listings, author affiliation, augmented keyword searching. Wallingford Oxon OX10 8DE, United Kingdom

(continued)

SPECIAL BIBLIOGRAPHIC NOTES

related to special journal issues (separates)
and indexing/abstracting

- ☐ indexing/abstracting services in this list will also cover material in any "separate" that is co-published simultaneously with Haworth's special thematic journal issue or DocuSerial. Indexing/abstracting usually covers material at the article/chapter level.

- ☐ monographic co-editions are intended for either non-subscribers or libraries which intend to purchase a second copy for their circulating collections.

- ☐ monographic co-editions are reported to all jobbers/wholesalers/approval plans. The source journal is listed as the "series" to assist the prevention of duplicate purchasing in the same manner utilized for books-in-series.

- ☐ to facilitate user/access services all indexing/abstracting services are encouraged to utilize the co-indexing entry note indicated at the bottom of the first page of each article/chapter/contribution.

- ☐ this is intended to assist a library user of any reference tool (whether print, electronic, online, or CD-ROM) to locate the monographic version if the library has purchased this version but not a subscription to the source journal.

- ☐ individual articles/chapters in any Haworth publication are also available through the Haworth Document Delivery Services (HDDS).

Japanese Distribution Channels

CONTENTS

ABOUT THE EDITOR

Takeshi Kikuchi is Professor of Marketing at the Science University of Tokyo, Japan. He is a highly regarded authority on Japanese marketing theory and practice. His background includes extensive experience as an executive for several multinational corporations and as a widely sought-after consultant in numerous countries around the world. Takeshi Kikuchi's extensive contacts with academic marketing colleagues in Japanese universities and research institutes and the high esteem in which he is held by them are what made it possible for him to assemble such a distinguished group of authorities on Japanese distribution channels.

Preface

This is a *very* special collection. For the first time, Japanese distribution channels–a topic of great interest about which much has been written in recent years–are examined in depth by *Japanese* scholars. Takeshi Kikuchi of the Science University of Tokyo, the Editor for this volume, has done an outstanding job of assembling a group of scholars from some of Japan's leading universities and research institutes to present their work on Japanese distribution channels. All of the scholars whose work is presented in this book have not only studied and researched Japanese distribution channels for many years but they have *lived* with the distribution system as well. Indeed, as professionals and consumers, they have been exposed to the "ins and outs" of the system on a day-to-day basis throughout their lifetimes. The result is a collection of articles that provides not only great depth of knowledge but perspectives and insights that heretofore have not been available.

As the Editor of the *Journal of Marketing Channels* I am most grateful to all of the authors and the Editor for their outstanding contributions that make up this volume. The work presented here is unique and will stand for many years in the future as a major contribution to the literature on Japanese distribution channels.

Bert Rosenbloom

[Haworth co-indexing entry note]: "Preface." Rosenbloom, Bert. Co-published simultaneously in the *Journal of Marketing Channels* (The Haworth Press, Inc.) Vol. 3, No. 3, 1994, p. xv; and: *Japanese Distribution Channels* (ed: Takeshi Kikuchi) The Haworth Press, Inc., 1994, p. xiii. Multiple copies of this article/chapter may be purchased from The Haworth Document Delivery Center [1-800-3-HAWORTH; 9:00 a.m. - 5:00 p.m. (EST)].

Introduction

Japan is the world's second largest economy. It is a global leader in industrial production, manufacturing methods, and the application of sophisticated technology to a host of industries. The output of the vast Japanese economy is exported to all corners of the earth. Indeed, Japan has become recognized as an economic and industrial "powerhouse" in the international arena during the last several decades.

The dramatic transformation of the Japanese manufacturing sector into one of the world's most advanced has not been shared equally by Japan's distributive sector. But there have been substantial changes in distribution structure and processes in Japan over the past several decades. Unfortunately there are still many misconceptions about Japanese distribution channels that have been perpetuated by superficial analyses as well as myths that may have little basis in fact.

This special collection on Japanese distribution channels was developed to provide greater depth of insight into Japanese distribution channels than is currently available. Here the reader will find the work of Japanese marketing scholars who have in-depth and intimate knowledge of distribution in Japan. These researchers have not only closely studied these systems for many years and in numerous cases worked in them, but also as consumers have relied on these channels to meet their needs. This combination of scholarship in researching the distribution system along with experience from being involved in and using the system is an ideal synergy that I believe is unmatched in the existing literature on Japanese distribution channels.

The opening article of the publication by Yoshihiro Tajima, "Japan's Markets and Distribution System" offers a penetrating analysis of distribution channels in Japan. Tajima provides substantial insights into the difficulties of gaining access to Japanese markets via the distribution system not only for overseas businesses but for Japanese corporations as well.

The second article by Tatsuro Watanabe, "Changes in Japan's Public

[Haworth co-indexing entry note]: "Introduction." Kikuchi, Takeshi. Co-published simultaneously in the *Journal of Marketing Channels* (The Haworth Press, Inc.) Vol. 3, No. 3, 1994, pp. 1-2; and: *Japanese Distribution Channels* (ed: Takeshi Kikuchi) The Haworth Press, Inc., 1994, pp. 1-2. Multiple copies of this article/chapter may be purchased from The Haworth Document Delivery Center [1-800-3-HAWORTH; 9:00 a.m. - 5:00 p.m. (EST)].

Policies Toward Distribution Systems and Marketing," offers an in-depth analysis of the significant changes in government policies that are moving Japan towards less regulation while helping reduce monopoly powers. Watanabe's findings are based on a wide range of sources in Japan, both private and public and hence offer the most up-to-date and authoritative views on the topic.

Yutaka Kakeda examines thoroughly the changing structure of the Japanese distribution system in "Changes in Japan's Distribution Structure." Kakeda concludes that Japan's distribution channels, although still unique, have changed in recent years in ways that make them more similar to other advanced countries.

In "Three Methods to Deal with the Uncertain Market Environment: Establishing New Intrachannel Relationships," Takeshi Moriguchi offers some fascinating findings about processes occurring within Japanese distribution channels. Moriguchi finds that micromarketing, strategic information systems, and strategic alliances have become instrumental in fostering cooperative relationships in Japanese marketing channels.

Toshiaki Taga and Yukihiko Uehara delve into the rationale underlying relationships in Japanese distribution channels in "Some Characteristics of Business Practices in Japan." Their analysis goes a long way in clarifying some commonly held misconceptions about the operation and efficiency of transactions in Japanese distribution channels.

Finally, Yoshio Takahashi provides an analysis of the implications of the effect of a U. S. "category killer" on the structure and operation of marketing channels in Japan in "Toys "R" Us Fuels Changes in Japan's Toy-Distribution System." The findings concerning the structural changes and power shifts predicted to result from such giant retailers' entry into Japan might have far reaching effects on distribution channels for many other products in Japan.

As Editor for this volume on Japanese distribution channels I would like to express my deepest gratitude to the authors of the articles. They have done a truly outstanding job. I am highly honored and take deep pride in having had the opportunity to work with these colleagues in putting this special collection together. I would also like to express my thanks to the Editor of the *Journal of Marketing Channels*, Bert Rosenbloom, for inviting me to be the Editor for this book. I am hopeful that the collection of articles presented here will become a most valuable resource for academics, business practitioners, government officials, and anyone else who wants to gain a deeper understanding of the structure and dynamics of Japan's distribution channels.

Takeshi Kikuchi

Japan's Markets and Distribution System

Yoshihiro Tajima

SUMMARY. Japan's markets are very difficult to initially penetrate by overseas businesses as well as Japanese corporations. Among the various market impediments, greater attention should be focused on the fundamental problem–the distinctive feature of the markets and closed nature of the established distribution system in Japan. The country's exclusive nature was formed in the course of history with the evolution of its distribution structure, business practices and public intervention.

INTRODUCTION

Objectively speaking, Japan's markets are a tough nut to crack–not only for overseas businesses and products but also for Japanese corporations that are attempting to diversify into new partial markets or submarkets. Some submarkets are founded upon trade practices that differ from others and have an imperceptible but undeniably prevalent atmosphere inclined to shun new entries.

In the widening imbalance in trade with Japan, the United States, the European Community, and others have mounted pressure on Japan to lift market obstacles that deny overseas companies and products access to Japanese markets. Except in certain agricultural markets where there is strong domestic opposition, the Japanese government has made substantial efforts to encourage imports, particularly of manufactured products. This

Yoshihiro Tajima is Professor of Marketing at Gakushuin University and Chairman of the Japan Society of Marketing and Distribution.

[Haworth co-indexing entry note]: "Japan's Markets and Distribution System." Tajima, Yoshihiro. Co-published simultaneously in the *Journal of Marketing Channels* (The Haworth Press, Inc.) Vol. 3, No. 3, 1994, pp. 3-16; and: *Japanese Distribution Channels* (ed: Takeshi Kikuchi) The Haworth Press, Inc., 1994, pp. 3-16. Multiple copies of this article/chapter may be purchased from The Haworth Document Delivery Center [1-800-3-HAWORTH; 9:00 a.m. - 5:00 p.m. (EST)].

3

led to the rapid rise in the ratio of manufactured-product imports among the growing volume of imports in general (Table 1).

The ratio reached as high as almost 50% of the total imports in 1991, but still remains at a much lower level compared to other advanced countries, as shown in Table 2.

Growth, however, has seemingly reached its limit. Today, import-promoting measures that produce immediate effects can no longer be found. In particular, the recent economic slowdown has spurred an export drive. Combined with lethargic imports, trade surpluses reached an unprecedented high.

The Japanese themselves consider the huge trade surplus malapropos and are aware that it must be trimmed for Japan to survive as a respected member of the international economic community. In face of the fact that

TABLE 1. Recent Trends in Japan's Imports

(cif, customs clearance basis: US $ mil.)

Year	Total Imports (US $ mil.)	Index (1984 = 100.0)	Total of Products (US $ mil.)	Ratio in Total Imports (%)
1984	134,257	100.0	36,451	27.2
1985	127,512	95.0	35,822	28.1
1986	119,424	89.0	43,242	36.2
1987	146,048	108.8	59,429	40.7
1988	183,252	136.5	84,066	45.9
1989	207,356	154.4	98,279	47.4
1990	231,223	172.2	109,828	47.5
1991	234,102	174.4	112,948	48.2

Data: OECD Foreign Trade by Commodities

TABLE 2. Ratio of Products in Total Imports in Selected Countries

(as of 1991)

Country	JPN	US	UK	Germany	France	Italy	Canada
Products Total Imports (%)	48.2	76.7	77.8	76.2	76.4	67.4	82.9

Data: OECD

measures to promote imports have not necessarily won long-term success, Japan is making a serious effort to uncover the real reason why overseas businesses and products are unable to make substantial inroads into its markets.

Cultural factors such as the language and customs, as well as steep land prices and utility charges, have very often been cited as market impediments. Greater attention, however, should be paid to the more fundamental problem. This is the distinctive features of Japan's markets that have been cultivated down through history and the closed nature of the country's established distribution system. The exclusionary nature had been formed in the course of the history of building Japan's distribution structure, business practices, and public intervention in distribution activities (the legal and administrative framework of distribution).

This study tries to analyze the historical background and current state of the closed nature of Japan's markets and distribution system, and to briefly explore their future.

HISTORICAL BACKGROUND OF THE JAPANESE MARKET

Comparatively High Savings Rate

Notwithstanding Japan's surge into the top ranks in the area of income level, propensity to save remains comparatively high, and as its result, inevitably the ratio of consumption spending to disposable income stays at the lower level in comparison to other industrialized nations. The high saving or low spending level has become a major obstacle in increasing imports in general and in boosting imports of finished consumer goods in particular. From the overseas point of view, the domestic consumer market is not growing as anticipated (see Table 3).

In the past the high level of savings has been attributed to the relative inadequacy of Japan's social security system. In spite of improvements in unemployment and medical insurances, annuity, and other social security schemes, consumer spending has been impeded by the high savings, even though propensity to save has been slightly decreasing as a trend. Apparently one of its reasons is the big saving required for home purchase, an undertaking regarded by many to be the most important means of assurance. Moreover, the influence dies hard of Confucian ethics that emphasize the virtues of hard work and saving. Korea and Taiwan, both historically influenced by Confucianism, also show a higher saving rate. It is interesting for us, even though difficult to decide whether this is due to Confucian ethics or just to the developing stage of the economy.

TABLE 3. Household Disbursements in Japan, US and UK

(%)

Year	Japan		United States		United Kingdom	
	Propensity to consume	Propensity to save	Propensity to consume	Propensity to save	Propensity to consume	Propensity to save
1982	83.3	16.7	91.2	8.8	92.5	7.5
1983	83.9	16.1	93.0	7.0	94.4	5.6
1984	84.2	15.8	91.7	8.3	92.9	7.1
1985	84.4	15.6	93.4	6.6	93.4	6.6
1986	83.9	16.1	93.8	6.2	95.5	4.5
1987	85.3	14.7	95.6	4.4	97.5	2.0
1988	85.7	14.3	95.5	4.5	99.2	0.8
1989	85.4	14.6	95.9	4.1	97.8	2.2
1990	85.9	14.1	95.5	4.5	96.1	3.9
1991	85.0	15.0	95.1	4.9	94.3	5.7

Still, Japanese values are today moving slowly away from those upheld by traditional work ethics, toward enjoyment of life. Confucianism is losing its hold, particularly among young people.

Industrial Structure Oriented to Self-Sufficiency

The second distinctive characteristic of the Japanese market is self-sufficiency in the area of finished consumer goods. Japan can satisfy all of its domestic consumer needs. This system of self-sufficiency was formed through historical developments. Over the span of 300 years from the mid-sixteenth to mid-nineteenth centuries, Japan kept its doors closed to the outside world. Aside from limited trade with the Netherlands and China, Japan produced everything it needed and built a corresponding industrial structure.[1] After the Meiji Restoration of 1868, Japan aspired to become a trading nation, but only in the form of exporting processed goods. Japan wished to import raw materials and processing equipment from abroad and to export finished products. The low level of finished-goods imports was cultivated from that time. The mechanisms of self-sufficiency continue to persist in Japan. This proves that its industrial structure is not evolving toward a system founded upon the principle of international division of labor.

The Japanese Image of Imported Goods

While Japan remained closed, most of the items imported from the Netherlands and China were rare luxury items treasured by members of the high-ranking warrior class and rich merchants. Until recently, expensive imports were called "hakurai-hin" (merchandise brought in by ship). The term itself suggests the general Japanese view of imports. Since the Meiji Period, the Japanese have had a strong attachment to rare, expensive items–especially those from Europe–and looked to domestic products to meet everyday needs. In markets of daily necessities, imports were regarded as being cheap–but inferior to competitive Japanese products.

This self-sufficient structure cultivated over the centuries (particularly for finished consumer goods) and the consumer image toward imports are believed to be some of the very important impediments to market access.

The Direction of Change

Dramatic change is nevertheless on its way to alter the traditional features of the Japanese market. Since the collapse of the so-called "bubble economy," Japanese consumers have become sensitive to pricing, thus spurring retailers to wage a price competition. The more than 10 million Japanese who visit other countries every year gain firsthand experience and knowledge concerning the wide gap in consumer prices between Japan and other countries. Growth in overseas travel may be one of the major factors in the rising consumer demand to reduce the price gap.

The appreciation of the yen has also prompted Japanese manufacturers to move manufacturing operations to offshore locations. In the price wars, particularly to meet the rise of "category killers," leading retailers are adopting into their procurement strategy a system of so-called "development import." This means the manufacture of products according to Japanese specifications by overseas companies for import and marketing in Japan. Such developments, combined with the continuing rise of the yen, have encouraged imports of finished overseas products and may pave the way for greater international competition in the Japanese marketplace.

The number of consumers who prefer better goods, regardless of origin, is definitely increasing. Choice based on price is likely to add advantages for overseas products in a marketplace that is already working in imports' favor with foreign-exchange bargains.

STRUCTURAL CHARACTERISTICS
OF THE JAPANESE DISTRIBUTION SYSTEM

Old Practices Die Hard

A distribution system is part of a larger economic system created by each society, as are manufacturing and financial systems. As a product of historical development, it is natural for the Japanese system to acquire distinctive characteristics in the course of its formation. Yet, there exist no other distribution systems among advanced countries with such outdated characteristics still intact. The present American distribution system is similarly the product of historical development. The system, however, no longer shows the traces of Yankee peddlers on horseback or in wagons selling wares to frontiersmen far from the coast. In Japan, however, traditions that date far beyond those of America's peddlers still exist in the foundation of the Japanese system, reluctant to market-opening to the foreign and domestic newcomers.

Sales Channels Segmented by Product

Concerning Japan's distribution system, its vast number of shops and the diminutive size of average operations, so-called the excessive presence and Lilliputian scale, are usually cited in retailing. On the wholesale level, products flow through a number of layers of middlemen: one, two, or for some products even three. The stratified structure of the wholesale system has also been cited as to the backwardness of Japan's distribution system. They are undeniable facts but are not necessarily the direct causes of difficult market entrance.

The real problem in the distribution structure for foreign businesses and products in accessing the Japanese market is the highly segmented sales channels built for each product group. Let me elaborate with specific examples.

In New York and other large cities in the United States small street corner fruit shops can be seen. They are more of an exception, however, than part of the mainstream. The dominance of limited-line stores specializing in certain types of food–such as vegetables, fruit, meat, or processed foods–has become a thing of the past. Needless to say, the principal force in food distribution today is the general food retail operation represented by the supermarket chain and its variations. These large retailers supply all types of foods from fresh produce to processed foods, as well as toiletries and other nonfood products. Accordingly, all-round wholesalers have grown to supply the bulk of the product assortment for supermarkets. A single large channel thus supplies a wide variety of food products and other daily necessities to consumers.

In Japan, supermarkets, convenience stores, and other food retailers with a wider assortment have grown to dominate much of the food market especially in urban areas. Limited-line stores, however, selling fresh produce, seafood, meat, liquor and seasonings, and bread and confections remain overwhelmingly large in number. The same is true for areas other than foods (Table 4).

The wholesale level continues to retain the structure of segmentation by product type. For each type of limited-line store, there exists a corresponding limited-line wholesaler. For example, a bread-and-confectionery store is sup-

TABLE 4. Structure of Food Stores

	Japan (as of 1991)			USA (as of 1987)		
	Number of stores	Percentage Distribution		Number of stores	Percentage Distribution	
		Number of stores	Sales		Number of stores	Sales
Food stores	622,751	100.0%	100.0%	225,900	100.0%	100.0%
Grocery stores	68,913	11.1	39.5	137,584	60.9	89.0
Alcoholic beverage stores	106,650	17.1	15.3	35,194	15.6	5.8
Meat & poultry stores	28,792	4.6	3.3	11,364	5.0	1.8
Fish stores	41,204	6.6	4.0			
Dry food stores	8,141	1.3	0.8	–	–	–
Vegetable & fruit stores	46,700	7.5	4.9	3,271	1.3	0.6
Confectionery & bakery stores	126,194	20.3	7.4	27,914	12.5	1.9
Rice & cereals stores	37,098	6.0	4.6	–	–	–
Other retail food & beverage stores	159,059	25.5	20.2	10,573	4.7	0.9

Data: Japan–MITI's "Census of Commerce 1991" (Preliminary Report)
USA–1987 Census of Retail Trade, Bureau of Census

plied by a dedicated wholesaler. Liquor wholesalers supply alcoholic beverages and seasonings to retailers specializing in such products.

To sum up, no general wholesalers exist in Japan on the scale of Super Valu or Fleming of the United States, which are said to supply 70 percent or 80 percent of the product assortment of each supermarket. Japan's wholesale stage is composed of wholesalers of wide variety, each of which specializes in a specific category of merchandise. Although some leading wholesalers are making great efforts to expand the scope of their product lines in response to the growth of supermarkets and other large-scale retailers, various limitations, which will be discussed later, have impeded their success. As a result, even the most successful food wholesaler in Japan, which boasts the largest business scale and widest product diversity, has had to concentrate on alcoholic beverages, seasonings (such as soy sauce, miso paste, and vinegar), processed foods, snack foods, and preserves. This group of wholesalers normally does not carry fresh produce, seafood, meat, bread, and sweets. The company carries no toiletry or cosmetic products, let alone paper products or cigarettes.

Even the largest wholesaler can supply only a number of product categories from the 10,000 products an average supermarket offers. Product procurement for convenience stores, which sell 3,000 items on average, is also segmented into a number of wholesalers much larger than the number in the United States. Conditions differ only minimally for other consumer products. Distribution in Japan is founded upon numerous small and specialized sales channels (see Table 5).

The Historical Background

These structural features were developed through historical processes. Although this history of Japan's commerce need not be described in full, the major cause dates back to the "za" that was popular in the twelfth to sixteenth centuries' medieval period and the "kabu-nakama" system that flourished in the sixteenth to nineteenth centuries' Edo Period. The "za" group was an exclusionary cooperative of members in a single profession, which was granted various commercial privileges in exchange for service to leading shrines, temples, or influential leaders. The "za" was a group of artisans or merchants, separated by product type.[2] Without membership in a group for a specific product, nobody was permitted to sell the product. Because only single membership was allowed to a merchant, each vendor was forced to specialize in a single product category. The comparison of "za" with the European guild is an interesting topic for research. In the perspective of this study, it must be noted that they share structures as organizations aimed at dominance and exclusion of others in one area of trades.

TABLE 5. Structure of Food Wholesaling

Kind of business	Number of establishments
Farm, livestock & fishery products	43,331
Rice, barley & wheat	2,808
Grains & pulses	1,652
Vegetables	8,108
Fruits	3,439
Meat & Poultry	8,005
Fresh fish, shellfish & seaweed	14,624
Miscellaneous farm, livestock & fishery products	4,695
Food & beverages	56,656
Sugar	989
"Miso" & soy sauce "Shoyu"	1,415
Beer, wine & liquors	5,941
Dry food	6,878
Canned & bottled food (in airtight containers)	1,507
Bakery & confectionery products	8,475
Soft drink & carbonated water	3,266
Tea	3,519
Miscellaneous food & beverages	24,666

Data: MITI's "Census of Commerce 1991" (Preliminary Report)

In the transition from feudalism to the premodern period, the trade system was abolished. Commerce enjoyed a new latitude of freedom and vitality with the emergence of many daring and innovative merchants. With the onset of social stability, however, similar specialized and closed unions called kabu-nakama were organized. In return for financial contributions to the shogunate and to feudal lords, the unions were granted trade monopolies in their respective areas of business. The groups restricted the number of members and rigorously eliminated aspiring merchants. In this system, the product flow from producer to retailer was built according to the initiative of the wholesaler.

After 1868's Meiji Restoration, the new government ordered dismantling of the kabu-nakama system. The rigidly segmented and closed trade organizations disappeared and commercial freedom was guaranteed. Nevertheless, the characteristics of traditional distribution channels remain to this day without fundamental changes.

The distribution system comprises an organic social body consisting of product distributors. Distributors are interlinked by specialization and competition. Specialization may be vertical or functional (such as wholesale or retail) or by region or product category. The distribution system changes through competition and changes in these interrelationships.

In Japan, the growth of specialization created a complex distribution system. The development of za and kabu-nakama–plus similar exclusive unions formed after the Meiji Restoration (although these entities had lost their privileges)–discouraged competition. This was fostered also by the Japanese preference for stability.

CHARACTERISTICS AND CHANGES IN TRADE RELATIONS

Change in Distribution-Channel Leadership

The characteristics of Japan's distribution system were formed in the course of wholesalers' preponderance in distribution channels. This can be seen in many parts of the system. In the past, wholesalers monopolized warehouses and the means of transportation, such as ships and horses–hence reaping profits from the price difference between the production sites and the consumer market. By accumulating huge capital, the merchants were able to control the manufacturers and retailers. During the Edo Period, the city of Edo (present-day Tokyo) used gold as its currency, while Osaka used silver for trade. Because of the need for exchanging gold and silver–similar to the foreign exchange of today–many wholesalers performed this function. This led to their domination of financing in addition to product distribution. A number of today's banks and trading companies were incubated from such wholesalers.

Under the industrial revolution in the Meiji Period (1868-1912), a number of manufacturers were born around the year 1900. Still in their infancy, established wholesalers provided capital to these makers and assumed the job of selling the manufacturers' products as general nationwide distributors or regional sales agents. The wholesalers wielded control of retailers by product supply, distribution, and financing. Their power over production capital continued until the end of the Second World War. The close ties between manufacturers and wholesalers in the domestic market date back from such times.

In the postwar period, distribution-channel leadership for manufactured goods, particularly for branded consumer goods, moved from wholesalers to manufacturers. The introduction of innovative products as in the household appliance industry; mass production through automation; and the growth of mass marketing alongside the development of television, radio, newspaper, magazines, and other media, reversed the power relationship between manufacturers and wholesalers. Many makers were able to liberate themselves from wholesalers' control. In fact, they selected and set up wholesalers throughout Japan as sales agents to build their own marketing channels. Makers of durable consumer goods such as household appliances, over-the-counter drugs, high quality cosmetic products, and some toiletry products transformed wholesalers into exclusive sales companies through capital investment and manpower assistance, alongside the formation of networks of affiliated retailers.

The maker-led formation of sales channels also reinforced the exclusionary nature of the distribution system. Inasmuch as the system had historically been segmented by product category and corresponding sales channels, the action by leading makers to build their own marketing systems, by screening wholesalers and in some cases forming an exclusive channel to serve one company, had denied channel access to competing makers. That is why market access has been difficult not only for overseas companies and products but also for Japanese companies diversifying into other businesses.

Business Relationships and Practices

The insularity of Japan's markets derives not only from the structural characteristics of its distribution but also from business practices. Sociologists and cultural anthropologists have described Japan as a society based on human relationships rather than on contracts. In fact, stable, long-term human ties are regarded as having the greatest importance in business relations among manufacturers, wholesalers, and retailers. This situation has been described by some as Gemeinschaft rather than Gesellschaft. This is proven by some manufacturers who claim to have the same commitment as their marketing channels and to be "on the same boat."

Market access will undoubtedly be extremely difficult if such business relationships dominate. In addition, business practices also reinforce the closed nature of Japan's market. As a typically Japanese business practice, sales incentives (or deals) called "rebates" will be examined.

In the United States, makers offer volume discounts and cash discounts for large orders and early payment. This literally brings down the manufacturer's sales price. In Japan, sales to wholesalers who serve as sales agents are also based on list prices. Volume rebate of a certain percentage is granted to cumulative orders for six months or a year. The rebate rate rises progressively for most makers. Large procurement over a given period increases the rebate rate. In addition, the rebate is determined not only according to volume but also for a variety of factors, including promptness in payment and allegiance to the maker.

When the rebate system becomes as intricate as this, it not only becomes a way to distribute profits but also a method of controlling wholesalers and retailers. This encourages channel exclusiveness, and at the same time it possibly falls under price discrimination prohibited by the Antimonopoly Law.

Moreover, the rebate standards and payment methods have not been disclosed publicly. To assure the legality and transparency of relating, it must be standardized, simplified, and publicized. Other practices such as merchandise returns, consigned sales, and sales-assistants' provision must also be reexamined to open the market.

More recently, the progress in sophisticated information systems has spurred fears of such systems being employed as a new means to strengthen affiliated ties. These systems must be watched carefully to promote competition.

The Influence of Retail Business Development

Supermarkets began to develop rapidly in Japan in the late fifties, triggering the "distribution revolution." This, however, brought about no profound changes in Japan's distribution system. One cause of this failure was the peculiarities in the development of supermarkets in Japan. In the early days, supermarkets depended heavily upon wholesalers for product supply, physical distribution, and financing. Many makers refused direct sales to supermarkets and sold only through their sales agents, the wholesalers. Part of the reason was their dim view of the supermarket's growth potential. Even if the makers had wished to establish direct ties, such a decision would have involved disruption of the established business order and the danger of a boycott by wholesalers and retailers. In fact, manufacturers traditionally depended on wholesalers for physical distribution to retailers and would have had to build their own distribution system for direct sales to supermarkets, which would be impossible in terms of cost.

The supermarkets themselves opted to procure from wholesalers. One reason was that this procurement channel eliminated the need to set up their own distribution centers or to build logistic systems. Another was the possibility to pay for procurements in bills, which made credit liabilities available for use as working capital. The growth of supermarkets brought about shortening of sales channels and concentration of wholesalers, but not to the point of uprooting the wholesale system itself.

The growth of retail business was not limited to supermarkets alone. There can be seen two basic directions. One direction in growth was the development of retailers with extensive product lines, such as supermarkets, convenience stores, and department stores. In physical distribution, this development exposed the contradictions in the segmented wholesale channels. Under the traditional system the retailers had to deal with countless wholesalers, thus increasing work in order placement, merchandise acceptance, and other distribution-related duties–and pushing up costs. This promoted mergers and amalgamation of wholesalers in different industries and the rise of wholesalers with broader product lines.

The other direction in growth appeared more recently, with the rise of discounters. As economic growth slowed, consumers looked for better pricing and helped to foster the growth of discount stores. This has intensified the price battle among retailers, and is making rapid structural change and greater distribution efficiency inevitable. Manufacturers now face new challenges in their marketing channel strategy.

CONCLUSION: ISSUES IN PUBLIC POLICY

In Japan a wide variety of government mediation unseen in other industrialized countries can be found in distribution. One group of measures, such as the "Large-Scale Retail Store Law," was aimed at arrangement of the competitive relationships between large and small retailers. Another group was designed to modernize the small and medium businesses that constitute most of the distributors. There is another group of laws to regulate distribution activity in the general regulations concerning specific products or industries. The laws and administrative measures based on these laws, except for those aimed at modernization of distributive businesses, in effect appeased competition in general and deterred progress in development of the distribution system.

The laws and administrative ordinances pertaining to distribution are expected to be revised in accordance with domestic public opinion and outside pressure such as the Structural Impediments Initiative. Reinforcement of the Antimonopoly Law is also promoting competition in distribution.

Government intervention was implemented because of the recognition, particularly strong in the legislature and the administration, that government guidance is necessary to place Japan in line with other advanced nations. Premodern features still die hard after only a century of opening to the outside world, even amid postwar economic growth.

Japan has nevertheless become one of the most powerful nations in the world. Government intervention into the distribution system must now take a major turn. It must now direct its energies into the encouragement of competition, market opening, protection of the environment in regard to physical distribution, conservation of resources, and improvement of the social infrastructure concerning distribution (including standardization of EDI).

REFERENCES

1. Kojima, Keizo, "Industrial Renaissance in Edo," Chuokoron, 1989.
2. Sasaki, Ginya, "Roots of Japanese Merchants," Kyoikusha, 1981.

Changes in Japan's Public Policies Toward Distribution Systems and Marketing

Tatsuro Watanabe

SUMMARY. The purpose of this thesis is to clarify the frameworks of Japan's public policies toward distribution systems and marketing, and to analyze changes in these policies and their impacts on business. Inasmuch as the momentum provided by the SII talks has spawned a series of measures, the general drift of administrative policy has shifted dramatically in favor of deregulation and efforts to strengthen the nation's antimonopoly legislation. This paper is based not only on literature that is presented in the references, but also on much literature in Japanese and on primary data from private and public sectors that are not included in the references.

SCOPE OF THE POLICIES AND THEIR CHANGES

Goals of the Policies

It is generally said that government intervention in economic processes and activities is inevitable to avoid market failure. Bureaucrats thus devote much attention to regulating and promoting industries to complement

Tatsuro Watanabe is Associate Professor of Marketing, Niigata University.
Address correspondence to: Tatsuro Watanabe, The College of Commerce of Niigata University, 2-746 Asahimachi-Dori, Niigata City, 951 Japan.

[Haworth co-indexing entry note]: "Changes in Japan's Public Policies Toward Distribution Systems and Marketing." Watanabe, Tatsuro. Co-published simultaneously in the *Journal of Marketing Channels* (The Haworth Press, Inc.) Vol. 3, No. 3, 1994, pp. 17-33; and: *Japanese Distribution Channels* (ed: Takeshi Kikuchi) The Haworth Press, Inc., 1994, pp. 17-33. Multiple copies of this article/chapter may be purchased from The Haworth Document Delivery Center [1-800-3-HAWORTH; 9:00 a.m. - 5:00 p.m. (EST)].

market mechanisms. Most developed countries, therefore, tend to intervene in such sectors as agriculture, mining and manufacturing. Only a few countries, however, have a specific policy regarding distribution systems and marketing (Boddewyn and Hollander 1972).

For example, in the United States there are no systematic federal government policies directed toward distribution and marketing, except antitrust and consumer-protection policies. This is because the policies in America are strongly influenced by four key ideas: federalism, laissez-faire, competition, and the concept of retailing as a residual (Boddewyn and Hollander 1972). To implement these four ideas, both federal and state antitrust acts have been strictly enforced. Much of the pertinent literature, therefore, has focused on antitrust issues (e.g., Grether 1966; Stern and Eovaldi 1984).

Conversely, the government of Japan has specific policies regulating and promoting these sectors. These policies are Japanese-style industrial ideas known as targeting policies (Woronoff 1992), and have been one of the critical issues between Japan and overseas countries.

The criteria of distribution systems and marketing are said to be efficiency, fairness, and consumer-orientation (Cox, Goodman, and Fichandler 1965). In Japan it seems that the policies have four goals: (1) promoting fair competition through establishing and maintaining the rule of competition; (2) improving efficiency and productivity in distribution systems and marketing; (3) improving the convenience of transactions including consumers; and (4) ensuring the equity of the allocation of performances.

These policy objectives, however, are recognized to be insufficient because they have been criticized both domestically and internationally. As a result, the following are presently taken into consideration as significant factors: (1) international harmonization, which means deregulation and promoting enhanced competition; (2) ensuring the interests of consumers, which means shifting to more consumer-oriented policies; and (3) introducing the standpoint of city planning and environmental protection.

Range of Policies

To achieve these objectives, many measures have been implemented. These include general and special facilitating laws, ordinances, and administrative guidances. These are enforced by the national, prefectural, and municipal governments. Guidance includes the following.

A. Policies promoting fair competition. A typical statute is the Antimonopoly Act, whose objectives are not only distribution systems and marketing, but also market structures and activities as a whole. It has been pointed out that the market structure is comprised of five factors: (1) the degree of concentration among competing sellers; (2) the degree of concentration among competing buyers; (3) the characteristics of products and production; (4) the conditions of entry into the market; and (5) the conditions of demand, use, and buying (Grether 1966). Government policies tend to monitor these five factors and activities in the marketplace to maintain the rule of competition, and to ensure the interests of consumers.

B. Policies promoting small- and medium-sized distributors (e.g., retailers and wholesalers) by financial and fiscal measures. The policies since the late sixties', that were in the past intended to protect distributors, have tended to modernize and rationalize them as independent participants of marketplace competition, and to avoid market failure. These policies are typically administered by the Small and Medium Enterprise Agency that maintains comprehensive measures in this regard (Small and Medium Enterprise Agency, MITI 1991).

C. Policies for coordinating commercial activities between large-scale retailers and small- and medium-sized retailers. These policies, which are based on the idea that it is imperative to avoid market failure in spite of the policies for promoting small- and medium-sized retailers, are designed to ensure fair opportunities for them.

D. Policies for equipping the infrastructures of distribution systems by upgrading and increasing distribution efficiency. The infrastructures typically include large-scale facilities for physical distribution (e.g., highway systems, airports, harbors, and complexes of physical-distribution facilities). Government intervention and promotion are needed in these fields to complement the market mechanisms because infrastructures cannot be satisfactorily equipped only through market mechanisms.

E. Policies for regulating specific industries or products. Laws are enacted to regulate specific industries or products (e.g., liquor, rice, pharmaceuticals, and gasoline). These laws widely influence product distribution and marketing through licensing or permit systems, taxation systems, and other measures, although the laws have other goals besides the dedicated objectives of policies toward distribution systems and marketing.

The policy ranges have been changing along with changes in the priorities of the objectives. The focuses of the policies have thus been shifting dramatically in favor of deregulation and efforts to strengthen the nation's antimonopoly legislation.

Impacts of the SII Talks

As stated above, Japan's public policies toward distribution systems and marketing are undergoing transition, because they have been criticized domestically and internationally. During much of the Japan-U.S. Structural Impediments Initiative (the SII talks) that began in September 1989, the American representatives took issue with the closed nature and opaqueness of Japan's markets, and the absence of a level playing field for imported goods and foreign firms striving to compete here. As set out in the final reports concluding the SII talks in June 1990, Japan pledged to take corrective action at an early date, and attended a follow-up meeting to survey the progress made (U.S.-Japan Working Group 1990).

The SII talks thus provided key momentum for a sweeping transformation in public policies. This policy shift is centered chiefly upon efforts to overhaul legislative frameworks that block market access, and to revamp or replace business practices that are exclusionary or opaque. These can be understood in effect to be policies for an open marketplace.

Characteristics of the policy shift are shown by two government actions. The first was implemented by the Ministry of International Trade and Industry (MITI) regarding the regulation on the establishment of large-scale retail stores (LSRSs). The second is implemented by Japan's Fair Trade Commission (JFTC) regarding antimonopoly administration. These reflect two key concepts: (1) international harmonization and (2) ensuring the interests of consumers. Following is an overview of these.

REVISIONS TO THE REGULATION
ON THE ESTABLISHMENT OF LSRSs

Process of Revisions to the LSRS Law

Frameworks of the LSRS Law

The Large-Scale Retail Store Law (LSRS Law), that has restrictions on the establishment of LSRSs, was enacted in 1973. The LSRS law intends to ensure fair opportunities for small- and medium-sized retailers, while considering the interests of consumers.

Although the original LSRS law had applied to LSRSs having a minimum of 1,500 square meters of floor space, it was amended in 1979 to extend to LSRSs with floor space exceeding 500 square meters. The LSRS law applied not only to the establishment of new stores, but also to the expansion of floor space of established stores having more than 500 square meters of floor space.

Applications were formally to be reviewed by the LSRS Council. Applicants were to be recommended and ordered by the Minister of International Trade and Industry (in case of 1,500 (3,000) and above 1,500 (3,000) square meters: Category One) or each prefectural governor (in case of above 500 below 1,500 (3,000) square meters: Category Two).[1]

In actual fact, a substantial effect on the decision was wielded by the positions of the Council for Coordination of Commercial Activities (CCCA), which was organized under the local Chamber of Commerce and Industry (or Commerce and Industry Association) in each municipality. This is composed of local retailers, consumers, and people of academic standing. Moreover, the positions of the CCCA were mostly determined at the pre-meetings of the CCCA that comprised unofficial negotiations between local retailers and applicants. Consequently, although it was expected to take from one to two years in terms of the provisions of the LSRS Law itself, it took from three to five years and in some cases decision making took more than ten years to complete inasmuch as the unofficial negotiations had no time limits.

Owing to the actual enforcement of the LSRS Law, traditional small retailers had been protected from LSRSs. Moreover, it is more important that the LSRS law had reduced competition among such LSRSs as chain stores (Goldman 1991; Goldman 1992). Some researchers, however, have claimed in empirical studies that the LSRS Law has exerted only a small effect on Japan's retail structure (Flath 1990; Potjes 1993).

Three-Stage Program of Deregulation

The LSRS Law had been criticized that it made retail markets uncompetitive, and this was cited as a nontariff barrier to market penetration by foreign imports and foreign-affiliated retailers. Accordingly, the law damaged the interests of consumers, it was said. Therefore, MITI and its advisory counsels studied the implementation of more moderate deregulatory measures until 1989 (JCCI 1989; Takahashi 1989; Upham 1989). Overseas governments, however, such as the United States, could not be pleased with these gradual plans for deregulation. Ultimately, Japan pledged in the final SII report to implement a three-stage program of deregulatory measures.

The first stage, which was based on the interim report of the SII talks of April 1990, was initiated in May 1990 with revision to the implementation rules of the LSRS Law designed to streamline and relax the enforcement of certain stipulations, and to cut the time required for approval of new stores to 18 months.

The second stage of the deregulation process was followed a year later. In short, the administrative drive to revise the LSRS Law rested upon five pieces of legislation enacted in May 1991. These are discussed in the next Section.

As regards the third stage, it is mentioned in the amended LSRS Law itself that two years after the enforcement of the amended LSRS Law, the government of Japan will examine the provisions of the amended LSRS Law and the effectiveness of its implementation, including regulations applied to each local administrative area. Based upon this result, when necessary, Japan will take appropriate steps.

Enactment of the Five New Laws

The five pieces of legislation comprising revisions to the stipulation of regulation on establishment of LSRSs were presented in the earlier Section. Of these, (1) the Amendment to the LSRS Law and (2) the Special Law on Import Sales Space are designed to ease the restrictions imposed on the establishment of new stores. These two laws are designed to strengthen competition among LSRSs, and to promote international harmony and the interests of consumers.

As a measure to foster regional development, and to assist small- and medium-sized retailers, (3) the Law on the Development of Specific Shopping Centers is intended to clear the way for construction of shopping centers and integrated commercial-storefront districts. The third law introduces the standpoints of city planning and community protection. Two other laws, (4) the Amendment to the Law for the Promotion of Small and Medium Retail Business and (5) the Amendment to the Law for the Promotion of Private Enterprise, are conceived to provide financial backing for the development projects of specific shopping centers.

Amended LSRS Law

The Amendment to the LSRS Law, which was enforced in January 1992, has the following major components.

A. The introduction of a modified framework for processing new store applications. In essence, the LSRS Council is to expand its deliberations and the targets for its hearings. This means a strengthened framework for discussion and hearings by the LSRS Council; and the establishment of a new system of hearing the opinions of consumers, retailers, people of academic standing, and Chamber of Commerce and Industry (or Commerce and Industry Association). Other revisions were implemented to improve the deliberation process (Figure 1). First, the time frame for processing applications was limited to within one year at most. And sec-

FIGURE 1. Flow Chart of the Coordination Processing After Amendment of the LSRS Law

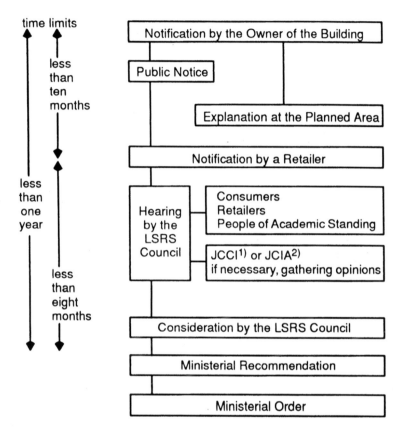

Note: 1. JCCI; The Japan Chamber of Commerce and Industry
2. JCIA; The Japan Commerce and Industry Association
Source: Data from MITI.

ond, the CCCA, which had been the chief body charged with processing applications, was abolished, and all duties involving deliberation of store applications were to be handled by the LSRS Council.

B. The relaxation of separate regulations by local public authorities. Many separate ordinances had been enacted by local public authorities, which had gone beyond the provisions of the LSRS Laws. There were two kinds of ordinances: ordinances that regulated the establishment of stores of less than 500 square meters, and ordinances that required the agreement of local communities, including local retailers, regarding all applicants. To ensure proper implementation, however, of separate regulations by local public authorities it is prescribed by the Laws that local public authorities should respect the objectives and outlines of the LSRS Laws. Consequently, most of the ordinances have been repealed, but some local public authorities have introduced new relaxed rules or guidelines.

C. The lifting of the floor-space criteria dividing Categories One and Two of the LSRSs. The floor space criteria of Category One of the LSRSs, which is submitted to the Minister of MITI, is raised from 1,500 (3,000) square meters and above 1,500 (3,000) square meters to 3,000 (6,000) square meters and above 3,000 (6,000) square meters. The criteria of Category Two of the LSRSs, which is submitted to the prefectural governor, is also lifted from above 500 square meters to less than 1,500 (3,000) square meters, to 500 square meters to less than 3,000 (6,000) square meters (see Note 1).

Special Law on Import Sales Space

The Special Law on Import Sales Space has been introduced under the LSRS Law to help satisfy international demands that Japan expand its level of imports. Essentially, the law allows LSRSs regulated by the LSRS Law to devote an initial maximum 1,000 square meters of contiguous floor space to the exclusive sales of imported items without being subject to regulation by the LSRS Law. Efforts, however, to establish new sales space for imported items have not developed the momentum initially anticipated.

Law on the Development of Specific Shopping Centers

The Law on the Development of Specific Shopping Centers was added out of consideration of the impact upon small and medium retailers of the amendment to the LSRS Law. The new Law's primary objective is to promote the retail business in general and smaller retailers in particular. The secondary objective, a key distinguishing feature of this legislation, is to encourage the formation of attractive urban environments and sound community growth. It is largely because of its second objective that this legislation is to be administered by three separate ministries: MITI, the Ministry of Construction, and the Ministry of Home Affairs. A special cooperative network for enforcement has been set up among the three ministries (Figure 2).

FIGURE 2. Flow Chart of the Law on Development of Specific Shopping Centers

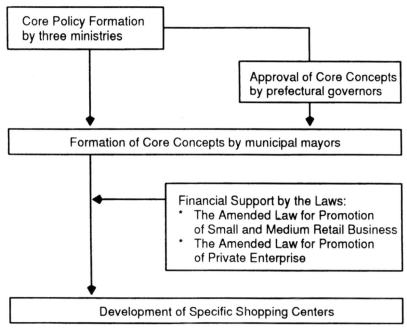

Source: Data from MITI.

This is almost the first time in Japan that the policies regulating the establishment of LSRSs introduce the standpoints of city planning and environmental protection, although the establishment of large-scale stores are regulated according to city planning and land-use control in Great Britain, Germany and the United States as a matter of course.

Effects of Deregulations and Future Prospects

The first stage of deregulation began in June 1990 with implementation of measures designed to relax enforcement of certain stipulations of the LSRS Law. From then through March 1991, 1,210 applications for establishing new retail outlets were made throughout Japan.[2] This figure is substantially above the annual average of 500 for the period between 1982 and 1989, when the role of administrative guidance had effectively limited new-store development. An unprecedented rush began to establish new stores following the last amendment of the LSRS Law in 1979.

Since March 1991, however, the volume of applications has settled back to levels prior to June 1990, suggesting that the sharp upturn may have only been a temporary phenomenon. In the half-year since the end of January 1992, when the amended LSRS Law went into effect, 432 applications for the establishments of new stores were submitted.[3] This and the other available data indicate that most large retailers are not only damaged by today's recession, but are also reviewing the siting strategies of their stores to correspond to strengthened LSRSs competition. These changes imply that they intend to introduce systems of both low-cost operation and low-cost investment, and to deal with the rapid progress of motorization. The following are typical of current trends.

Shifting the Location

This shift is of two forms. First, LSRSs already located in central business districts such as in existing commercial zones or around railway stations, are relocating to suburban areas and commercial zones along highways. The other directional shift is exemplified by an expanded volume of store applications for sites in local cities where administrative guidance has been repealed relating to the LSRS Law designed to subdue the development of LSRSs. These changes in siting strategies also include the closure and withdrawal from local markets of unprofitable stores that show no hope of improved performance.

Changes in Store Formats

Complementing the shift in siting toward suburban areas and commercial zones along highways are changes in store formats. Recent years have seen an impressive pace of development in discount-oriented stores known as power retailers or category killers. These comprise general discount stores, home centers, and mass-merchandisers of consumer electronics, toys, furniture, men's clothing, and automobile supplies. Wholesale clubs and outlet stores, which originated with American retailers, have also been opened. Some of them are foreign-affiliated retailers. They are planning to introduce low-cost operations to correspond to the increase in the number of price-conscious consumers; some of them take the EDLP strategy.

Beginning of the Shopping Center Age

There has been a growing number of projects to develop suburban regional malls and neighborhood shopping centers. Development work is also under way on integrated shopping centers with amenity facilities and power centers. To counter this trend and stage a competitive comeback, urban department stores located in central business districts have announced plans to expand new floor space. Many of these plans, however, are reexamined to cut down or withdraw, because they are affected by today's recession that is called the collapse of the bubble economy.

CHANGES IN THE ANTIMONOPOLY ADMINISTRATION

Strengthened Enforcement of the Antimonopoly Act

Reformation of Business Practices

Japan's Antimonopoly Act has been amended several times since 1947 when it was first enacted, modelling upon the Antitrust Acts in the United States. Traditional Japanese distribution systems and business practices, however, have also been cited as exclusionary and nontransparent to new market entrants including foreign businessmen.

These are related to the dominant characteristics of transactions in Japan: "transactions in intermediate organization." This is an intermediate form between market exchanges and transactions in internal organization.[4] Another term for this is administered vertical marketing systems (Stern and El-Ansary 1992). This form enjoys the merits of transactions within an internal organization (Williamson 1975). At the same time, it does not suffer from the inflexibility of transactions within an internal organization, inasmuch as it can enjoy the advantages of market exchanges.

This system, however, brings about problems of Japan's markets being cited as closed and exclusionary to newcomers. It has been pointed out that these problems are not mainly caused by the clauses of the Act itself but by its loose enforcement. This differs from the strict enforcement of the Antitrust Acts in the United States, which is shown in many cases relating to distribution systems and marketing (e.g., Howard 1983; Waldman 1978).

In response to criticism of these problems, and to encourage competition and strict compliance with the nation's antimonopoly administration, the JFTC established a set of new guidelines for enforcement of the Antimonopoly Act concerning distribution systems and business practices. Before the publication of the new guidelines, the draft was announced by JFTC in January 1991. After roughly half a year that included 60 days of hearings from concerned Japanese and U.S. government officials and the private sector, the final version was completed and enforced in July 1991. In addition, fines were increased for violations of the Antimonopoly Act.

In conjunction with these steps, MITI; the Ministry of Agriculture, Forestry, and Fisheries; the Ministry of Health and Welfare; and the Tax Administration Agency have held study-group or council meetings, and have come out with their own measures designed to reform business practices regarding the products over which they have administrative jurisdiction. In effect, work is under way to establish a framework for more acceptable and open business practices, including those outside the scope of antimonopoly legislation.

Overview of the Antimonopoly Act Guidelines

Given the desire to protect the interests of consumers and to ensure that Japan's markets are satisfactorily open and transparent to newcomers including foreign-affiliated companies, the purpose of the Antimonopoly guidelines is to eliminate closed and exclusionary distribution systems and business practices, and to see that market mechanisms are functioning properly. These goals are to be brought about through clearer interpretation and strengthened enforcement of the Antimonopoly Act.

The guidelines are comprised of three sections. Those in Section One chiefly deal with the continuity and exclusiveness of intercorporate trade, known as the long-term relationship between suppliers and customers (Taga and Uehara 1987). The guidelines focus upon business between producers and customers of capital and intermediate goods in particular. This business includes the following types of action: limiting competition to attract new customers, collective boycotts, and unfair reciprocal trade.

Section Two's guidelines are primarily concerned with trade among firms in the distribution sectors, and give special attention to transactions involving consumer goods, including the following: resale price maintenance, nonprice restrictions, and abuses of buying power by retailers.

Section Three provides guidelines on exclusive agency contract arrangements between competing firms not only for imports but for all products sold in the domestic market at large and on unfair obstructions to parallel imports.

The reasoning behind the guidelines is that they should serve as a compendium of conventional examples of applications that facilitate an easier grasp of the principles underlying the Antimonopoly Act. They are distinguished, however, by the fact that they provide stronger judgments as well as clearer judgmental criteria regarding specific types of practices.[5]

Reviewing Other Measures Relating to the Act

Overhauling the RPM Framework

Steps have also been taken to overhaul the resale price maintenance (RPM) framework. These remedial measures are designed to ensure that market pricing mechanisms function more effectively, and to stimulate price competition in the marketplace.

Since 1953 when the original Antimonopoly Act in 1947 was amended, the Law has granted several exemptions concerning the provisions of the ban on RPMs. Although the exemption lists in the Antimonopoly legislation were reduced, three exemption lines remained in 1992. For instance, (1) the Act exempted from applications of the Law RPMs on copyrighted books, magazines, newspapers, and records including compact discs (CDs) and music tapes. The JFTC also had compiled lists of items to be allowed to maintain resale prices, designating (2) 24 types of cosmetics and other toiletry items, each retailing for under ¥1030 inclusive of consumption tax, and (3) 26 types of pharmaceutical products for resale.

These systems have also been criticized for restricting the market pricing mechanisms. After the SII talks, the JFTC held study-group meetings about reexamining the RPM framework. As a result, several courses of action were taken: (1) imposing time limits on RPMs of CDs, which were to be permitted to maintain resale prices within two years after their initial purchase in November 1992, (2) 13 types of 24 types of cosmetics and 10 types of 26 types of pharmaceutical products were to be removed from the lists of RPMs in April 1993, and (3) vitamins and vitamin drinks were also slated for removal from the lists by the end of 1994.

Furthermore, the remaining items will be subject to review in 1998. It is already expected that the JFTC intends to phase out the RPM frameworks for all except copyrighted products, and to reduce the range of copyrighted products that are to be RPM-applicable.

Deregulation of Sales Promotion Activities

Sales promotion activities for consumers or customers, such as premiums and advertising, are regulated by the "Act Against Unjustifiable Premiums and Misleading Representations." This regulation is designed to ensure fair competition in the marketplace and to protect the interests of consumers.

Accordingly, steps have also been taken to revamp or loosen restrictions on these activities to ensure that they do not impede the participation of foreign firms and other market entrants. Restrictions have been eased on the use of premiums in promoting chocolate and other items, which were regulated by the Fair Competition Codes. And the ban on newspaper advertising with merchandise coupons, regulated by one of the Codes, has been lifted.

Although these measures have been taken, the regulations on sales promotion activities are criticized by foreign businessmen. For example, The American Chamber of Commerce in Japan in its White Paper 1993 calls for the replacement of the Act Against Unjustifiable Premiums and Misleading Representations (ACCJ 1993).

Influences of Policy Changes

Before the Antimonopoly Guidelines came out, manufacturers, whole-salers, and retailers in each industrial sector had launched efforts to bring their own business practices in line with the orientations set forth by MITI and other government ministries and agencies. These efforts intensified with the announcement of the Guidelines and have led to the initiation of practical reform programs. At the same time, many firms are beginning to set up compliance programs to encourage an improved understanding of the steps taken to beef up enforcement of the Antimonopoly Act. Some of the key accomplishments in the consumer goods areas are briefly discussed here.

Pharmaceuticals

The "discount compensation system" comprised ingrained business practices characterizing the medical pharmaceuticals business. In practice, manufacturers compensate wholesalers for discounts made on sales of pharmaceuticals to customers such as hospitals. Similarly, the pharmaceuticals business for consumers had been dominated by the "one store, one account" system, which limited retail pharmacies to only one wholesaler for supplies of a particular drug brand. These practices enabled manufacturers to exercise immense influence over the pricing of their products at each stage of the distribution process. Major revisions have been proposed, however, and headway is now being made toward the establishment of a pricing system that allows wholesalers and retailers to set their prices independently.

Toiletries and Cosmetics

Efforts have been moving ahead to streamline pricing structures and terms of trading in these markets. Some manufacturers have abolished rebate systems and adopted new trading policies. Steps have also been taken to base the delivery frequencies and other physical distribution criteria more clearly on purchase quantities and other business contract terms.

Groceries

In the groceries market, wholesalers have become increasingly outspoken in urging a fresh look at the nature of their business dealing with mass-merchandising operations such as supermarkets and convenience stores. Their complaints have had to do chiefly with product returns; high-frequency, small-lot, just-in-time deliveries; and the supply of labor to retail outlets and retailers' distribution centers. The Antimonopoly Guidelines have provided stronger regulatory controls to prevent retailers from abusing their buying powers. Many retailers, therefore, have been reforming their business practices.

Consumer Electronics

In this field, steps for manufacturers to streamline rebate systems and pricing structures began in the late eighties. Other practices such as sending company employees to work as sales helpers in mass-merchandisers are also up for revision.

Liquor

In the liquor business, brewers and distillers have long wielded key influence over the setting of prices at each stage of distribution. Today, however, beer advertisements often include the disclaimer, "Retail prices of beer are not regulated," which is a reaction to a JFTC directive, because many people believe that liquor retail prices are controlled by the government. In addition, the monitoring of activities such as unfairness to liquor discounters and predatory pricing have been stepped up.

Apparel

In the apparel industry, the nature of business dealing with department stores and mass-merchandisers has also come under scrutiny. The return of unsold goods and the sending of company employees to work as sales helpers in retail outlets are now under particular consideration for overhaul.

CONCLUSIONS

As the foregoing suggests, the momentum provided by the SII talks has spawned a series of measures designed to heighten the openness, transparency, and fairness of Japan's domestic distribution framework over the past years. The general drift of administrative policy has shifted dramatically in favor of deregulation and strengthening of the nation's antimonopoly legislation.

Inspired by developments on the administrative front, Japanese manufacturers, wholesalers, and retailers alike are charting practical new courses of action that will help prepare them for an era of increasingly intensified competition and global interdependence in the field of trade.

These developments appear certain to make the Japanese distribution systems and business practices more free and competitive, while at the same time offering new market entrants, including foreign-affiliated companies, expanded opportunities in Japan's marketplace.

Consequently, these policy changes reflect the shift in priority of the objectives of the policies presented at the beginning of this thesis. Japan's policies are undergoing a transition from the frameworks of policies that grant priority to production-oriented industrial policies, to frameworks that grant priority to (1) international harmony and (2) ensuring the interests of consumers. With regard to (3) introducing the standpoints of city planning and environmental protection, the first step is just being taken.

NOTES

1. Numbers in parentheses indicate large cities designated by the government.
2. Data from MITI.
3. Data from Nikkei Ryuutuu Shimbun, August 4, 1992.
4. There is much literature in Japanese on transactions within intermediate organizations, although it is not presented in the references.
5. The guidelines state which acts are "per se illegal," and which ones demand assessments of their impact on market competition as the criteria for "rule of reason."

REFERENCES

ACCJ: The American Chamber of Commerce in Japan (1993), *United States-Japan Trade White Paper 1993*.

Boddewyn, J. J. and S. C. Hollander (eds) (1972), *Public Policy toward Retailing*. MA: D.C. Heath and Company.

Cox, R., C. S. Goodman, and T. C. Fichandler (1965), *Distribution in a High-Level Economy*. NJ: Prentice-Hall.

DEI: The Distribution Economics Institute of Japan (1990), *Statistical Abstract of Japanese Distribution*.

Flath, D. (1990), Why are there so many retail stores in Japan?, *Japan and the World Economy, 2*, 365-386.

Goldman, A. (1991), Japan's Distribution System: Institutional Structure, Internal Political Economy, and Modernization, *Journal of Retailing, 67*, 154-183.

_____ (1992), Evaluating the Performance of the Japanese Distribution System, *Journal of Retailing, 68*, 11-39.

Grether, E. T. (1966), *Marketing and Public Policy*. NJ: Prentice-Hall.

Howard, M. C. (1983), *Antitrust and Trade Regulation*. NJ: Prentice-Hall.

JCCI: The Japan Chamber of Commerce and Industry (1989), *Distribution System and Market Access in Japan*.

Potjes, J. C. A. (1993), *Empirical Studies in Japanese Retailing*, Amsterdam: Thesis Publishers.

Small and Medium Enterprise Agency, MITI (1991), *Outline of Small and Medium Enterprise Policies of the Japanese Government*.

Stern, L. W. and T. L. Eovaldi (1984), *Legal Aspects of Marketing Strategy*. NJ: Prentice-Hall.

_____ and A. I. El-Ansary (1992), *Marketing Channels*, 4th ed., NJ: Prentice-Hall.

Taga, T. and Y. Uehara (1987), Japanese Business Practices. Working Paper, The Wharton School.

Takahashi, M. (1989), Provisional Summary of MITI's "Vision for the Distribution System in the 1990's," Working Paper, MITI.

Upham, F. K. (1989), Legal Regulation of the Japanese Retail Industry: The Large Scale Retail Stores Law and Prospects for Reform, Working Paper, The Program on U.S.-Japan Relations, Boston College Law School.

U.S.-Japan Working Group (1990), *Joint Report of the U.S.-Japan Working Group on the Structural Impediments Initiative*, June 28.

Waldman, D. E. (1978), *Antitrust Action and Market Structure*, MA: D. C. Heath and Company.

Williamson, O. E. (1975), *Markets and Hierarchies*, NY: The Free Press.

Woronoff, J. (1992), *Japanese Targeting*, London: The Macmillan Press.

Changes in Japan's Distribution Structure

Yutaka Kakeda

SUMMARY. The Japanese distribution system, when compared with other advanced countries', is highly unique. Its structural changes in recent years, however, have strengthened the similarity with advanced nations. In this paper I will outline a long-term view of structural changes in Japan's retail industry and clarify the opening-and-closure structure of retail stores.

INTRODUCTION

Starting with implementation of the first national survey of the Census of Commerce in 1952, such pioneering studies were conducted as Suzuki and Yamanaka (1962) and Arakawa (1962). In later years many researchers studied Japan's distribution system. According to their studies, a characteristic of Japan's distribution system was the existence of a large number of petty and occupational retailers and of multilevel wholesale transactions in comparison with other advanced countries. Overseas researchers also arrived at a nearly identical conclusion (e.g., Czinkota, 1985; Goldman, 1991). Especially during the rapid economic-growth period, when the inefficiency of Japan's distribution system was widely discussed, the scale of retail stores became larger through the development of supermarkets (Hayashi, 1964). Large retail corporations started to ap-

Yutaka Kakeda is Associate Professor of Marketing, Chiba University of Commerce. The author has an MBA from Keio University.

Address correspondence to: Chiba University of Commerce, c/o Yutaka Kakeda, 1-3-1 Kounodai, Ichikawa-shi, Chiba 272.

[Haworth co-indexing entry note]: "Changes in Japan's Distribution Structure." Kakeda, Yutaka. Co-published simultaneously in the *Journal of Marketing Channels* (The Haworth Press, Inc.) Vol. 3, No. 3, 1994, pp. 35-56; and: *Japanese Distribution Channels* (ed: Takeshi Kikuchi) The Haworth Press, Inc., 1994, pp. 35-56. Multiple copies of this article/chapter may be purchased from The Haworth Document Delivery Center [1-800-3-HAWORTH; 9:00 a.m. - 5:00 p.m. (EST)].

pear through the introduction of chain operations (Satou, 1971). The growth of supermarkets and advent of retail enterprises having sales of more than ¥2 trillion occurred during these two decades. Despite this, the aforementioned characteristic can still be recognized today. This demonstrates the peculiar nature of Japan's distribution system in comparison with other advanced countries. While in other such nations a large number of petty retailers and wholesalers were eliminated during the growth process of chain stores–such as supermarkets and the concentration into large retail enterprises–Japan has developed its distribution system by preserving petty retailers and wholesalers. This is a remarkable characteristic of Japan's distribution system (Goldman, 1991; Kakeda, 1992).

Several factors have been pointed out as causes that allowed the formation of a distribution system having both modern and traditional aspects. First, because the growth period of large retail enterprises coincided with the period of remarkably rapid economic expansion, a market size that enabled small retailers and wholesalers to survive was maintained despite the pressure of growing large-scale enterprises (Tamura, 1986).

Second, innovative retail businesses expanded by utilizing Japanese business practices such as rebates, the system of returning unsold goods, and excessive dealer helps. As a result, such business practices–the so-called business foundation of petty retailers and wholesalers–have been retained without renovation (Shimaguchi, 1977).

Third, chain stores in Japan placed their highest priority on investing in shops, and remained dependent upon the wholesale industry in distribution functions. This resulted in imperfect development of chain-store operations. The growth of chain stores, instead of cutting down the number of wholesalers, provided opportunities for wholesalers' proliferation. Petty retailers who were connected with such wholesalers therefore managed to survive.

Fourth, in addition to the more exclusive "keiretsu" system, almost all retailers and wholesalers formed a less-restrictive organization: the "cho-ai" system. The appearance of large retail enterprises did not necessarily bring about exclusion of the wholesale industry because long-term business relations and qualifications for dealings were observed (Shimaguchi and Lazer, 1979; Kakeda, 1992; Manifold, 1993).

Fifth, the population density of Japan's urban areas was extremely high. Although suburbanization of the population occurred, large shopping centers were seldom constructed in the suburbs because of the urban structural and road situations. Competition over space between urban centers and suburban areas was relatively mild. This enabled petty retailers in cities to survive amid highly dense populations.

Sixth, Japanese consumers demanded retail services of a high level (Goldman, 1992), and preferred perishable foods. Such tendencies are attributable to more frequent shopping visits by Japan's consumers than customers in Europe and the United States (Sharma and Dominguez, 1992). This enhanced the viability of small retailers who were more dependent upon neighborhood business.

Finally, the Large-Scale Retail Store Law that regulated the establishment of large stores was enacted in 1978 (the Department Store Law was in effect prior to this law). Moreover, the central and local governments in Japan prescribed a variety of distribution policies that restricted competition based on such laws as the Liquor Law and Pharmaceutical Law. Such ordinances indirectly regulated the establishment of retail stores (Czinkota and Woronoff, 1986; Suzuki, 1993). These policies seemed to have resulted in preserving small retailers whose competition was marginal.

The aforementioned factors seemed to have interdependently affected the development of the unique Japanese distribution system that is nonexistent in other advanced countries. In recent years, however, changes have been conspicuous in Japan's distribution system, especially in its structural aspects. The characteristics of the distribution system mentioned in the past have become highly diluted as was clearly demonstrated by the massive reduction in retail stores in 1985. The purpose of this paper is (a) to clarify the direction of such changes in the distribution structure with a focus upon retailing–the industry that has been undergoing the greatest changes–and (b) to conduct a dynamic analysis of the opening-and-closure structure of retailers that has brought about these changes.

DIRECTION OF RETAIL STRUCTURAL CHANGES

Decline in the Number of Retail Stores

According to the 1991 Census of Commerce, there were 1,591,223 retail stores in Japan, a decrease of some 28,000 in comparison with the previous survey of 1988. The retail industry consistently proliferated its number of outlets until 1982, except in 1962 when the number dwindled by some 16,000. Since 1985 when a great reduction of about 93,000 stores occurred, the number of shops continued to diminish despite the expanded survey subjects.[1] The declining tendency of retail stores seems to have stabilized.

One of the reasons for the decrease in retail stores is an increase in the shutdown of retailers who could not cope with environmental changes or who, because of poor business, lost their motivation to continue. More influential reasons for the decline are an increase in natural withdrawals owing to lack of successors. Other factors are hindrances to opening businesses because of surging land prices and rents, growing demand for advanced managerial ability, etc. The retail industry has long been described as "a source of income of last resort to the chronically unemployed and underemployed" (Sharma and Dominguez, 1992, p. 8). The declining tendency of retail stores will continue in the meantime, largely owing to such structural issues as a relatively reduced number of prospective retailers about to enter the retail market. In Japan the per capita number of retail stores is still larger than in other advanced countries. The dramatic changes that these countries underwent a few decades ago seem presently to be under way in Japan (Table 1).

Decrease in Petty Retailers

The retail industry, of course, mainly consists of establishments making sales to consumers. Because consumer spending is always strictly constrained, the retail industry's sphere of commerce cannot help being confined. The structure of the retail industry is naturally small compared with the wholesale industry. Stores with a maximum of two employees accounted for 53.2 percent in 1991. When stores with three or four employees were added to this figure, the total became 79.4 percent, indicating that most shops were petty operations with no more than four employees. The pettiness of our retail outlets is obvious. As was clearly recognized when compared with the 63.9 percent in 1970, the proportion of stores with a maximum of two employees has been rapidly dropping. The proportion of small outlets with three to four employees grew from 22.5 percent to 26.2 percent, and those with five to nine employees rose from 9.6 percent to 13.4 percent. The decline in petty outlets seems to be based on the diminished number of retail stores with one or two employees, and by an increase in shops that employ part-timers enabled by the prevailing part-time market of housewives and university students. (See Table 2.)

Retailing's occupational nature and pettiness are well-established. Table 3 shows the percentages of stores classified by type of legal organization. Incorporated establishments such as companies and cooperatives accounted for only 35.5 percent in 1991, and unincorporated establishments held the majority with 64.5 percent. Among unincorporated establishments, those without any regular employees were 42.9 percent. These figures demonstrate the occupational nature of retailing.[2] Considering, however, that in 1970, unincorporated establishments stood at 83.9 percent and that the ratio of unincorporated establishments with no regular employees dropped 30.9 points from 73.8 percent, the declining tendency of this occupational category has been steadily advancing.

TABLE 1. Changes in the Number of Retail Stores

(in thousands)

Year	1970	1972	1974	1976	1979	1982	1985	1988	1991
Number of shops	1,471	1,496	1,548	1,614	1,674	1,721	1,628	1,619	1,591
Growth rate	1.3	0.8	1.7	2.1	1.2	0.9	−1.8	−0.2	−0.6

(Note) Annual average growth rate in use
(Material) Census of Commerce Table

39

TABLE 2. Structural-Ratio Changes in the Number of Retail Stores by Scale

(%)

Year Number of employees	1970	1972	1974	1976	1979	1982	1985	1988	1991
0 – 2	63.9	62.0	62.5	61.9	61.1	60.2	57.7	54.0	53.2
3 – 4	22.5	23.3	23.3	23.7	24.0	24.0	25.1	26.1	26.2
5 – 9	9.6	10.5	10.2	10.3	10.5	10.9	11.7	13.2	13.4
10 – 49	3.7	3.9	3.7	3.8	4.1	4.6	5.1	6.3	6.6
50 +	0.3	0.3	0.3	0.3	0.3	0.4	0.4	0.5	0.5

(Material) Census of Commerce Table

TABLE 3. Structural-Ratio Changes in the Number of Retail Stores by Legal Organization

(%)

Year Legal Organization	1970	1972	1974	1976	1979	1982	1985	1988	1991
Incorporated (establishment)	13.1	17.8	19.0	20.6	22.8	25.3	27.6	31.1	35.5
Unincorporated (establishment)	83.9	82.2	81.0	79.4	77.2	74.7	72.4	68.9	64.5
(With no regular employees)	73.8	66.2	65.4	63.6	56.4	58.8	54.5	41.4	42.9

(Material) Census of Commerce Table

Decrease in Food-and-Drink Retail Stores

As Table 4 shows, one of the major characteristics of Japan's retail structure is that food-and-drink retail outlets are extremely large in number. Such shops accounted for 39.1 percent as of 1991, the largest percentage in the retail industry.

Whereas such retailers were greatly reduced in number in tandem with the growth of supermarkets in other advanced nations, these retailers have survived to a large extent in Japan. Their declining tendency, however, in terms of percentage has been accelerated, showing a diminution of about 112,000 stores from 1979 when the number of food-and-drink retailers reached its peak. Dramatic changes in recent years in Japan's retail structure have been triggered principally by food-and-drink retailers. (See Table 5.)

Let us look at more details in the trend by further classifying food-and-drink retail outlets into grocery stores, fresh food stores, manufacturing-retail food stores, and other food stores.[3]

The proportion of grocery stores among total outlets in 1991 was just 11.1 percent, but the percentage of total sales was the highest with 39.6 percent. This demonstrated that the scale of grocery stores was relatively large in comparison with other food-and-drink retailers. Fresh-food outlets were 18.7 percent in number and 12.2 percent in sales volume. These shops were relatively small in scale and have rapidly lost market share since 1979. Manufacturing-retail food outlets held similar percentages as fresh-food stores in the number of shops and amount of sales with 17.8 percent and 12.2 percent, respectively. Manufacturing-retail food outlets, however, were consistently increasing their percentages up to that point and could be described as a growing retailing segment amid a stagnant food market. Although other food stores held more than half the market in number of stores with 52.4 percent, their total-sales proportion was just 36.8 percent. Because each of the percentages showed a tremendous drop, other food outlets were gradually being reduced in significance in the food-and-drink retail market.

The transition of percentages in the number of food-and-drink retail stores and the amount of sales are illustrated in the previous tables. It was clearly demonstrated that in manufacturing-retail food outlets, the increase in the shop percentage preceded the increase in annual sales. In fresh-food stores and other food shops, the decrease in the percentage of annual sales preceded the decrease in the percentage of outlets. When the life cycle of each business type was assumed, interesting phenomena were observed. In a growth period the opening of small stores was accelerated, and in a declining period the delayed closure of marginal stores was detected.

TABLE 4. An International Comparison of Food Versus Nonfood Distribution Structures

	Japan 1985			US 1982			UK 1984			France 1987		
	All Retail	Food	Non-Food	All Retail	Food	Non-Food	All Retail	Food	Non-Food	All Retail	Food	Non-Food
Number of stores (000)	1,629	671	957	1,731	165	1,566	343	107	136	565	191	374
Stores per 1,000 persons	13.4	5.5	7.9	7.5	0.7	6.8	6.1	1.9	4.2	10.3	3.5	6.8
Stores per 10Km²	43.1	17.8	25.3	1.8	0.17	1.63	14.0	4.4	5.6	10.0	3.4	6.6

(Material) Goldman (1991), P. 159

TABLE 5. Structural-Ratio Changes in the Number of Retail Stores by Business Category

(%)

Year	1970	1972	1974	1976	1979	1982	1985	1988	1991
Assorted merchandise	0.2	0.2	0.2	0.2	0.2	0.2	0.2	0.2	0.3
Fabrics, clothing, personal articles	13.8	13.8	14.0	14.1	14.2	14.1	14.1	14.6	15.1
Food-and-drink merchandise	48.3	47.6	46.6	45.4	43.9	42.1	41.2	40.4	39.1
Automobiles, bicycles	4.0	4.0	4.0	4.2	4.4	4.9	5.2	5.5	5.9
Furniture, fixtures, utensils	10.6	10.5	10.6	10.9	10.9	11.0	10.6	10.3	9.9
Other	23.1	24.0	24.6	25.3	26.4	27.6	28.7	29.0	29.6

(Material) Census of Commerce Table

Growth of General-Assortment Stores

When general-assortment stores and limited-assortment stores are compared, the former enjoy a larger retail-market share of sales. Department stores, for example, have been growing in the sales of fabrics, clothing and personal articles[4]–steadily increasing market share from 23.8 percent in 1962 to 35.2 percent in 1991. The share of limited-assortment stores, however, decreased from 72 percent to 59.7 percent.

In the food-and-drink market, limited-assortment stores demonstrated a more striking decline in market share, their 84.4 percent of 1962 dropping to 52.0 percent in 1991. Although slight recovery occurred since 1985, the market share of limited-assortment stores declined, recording 46.0 percent in 1985, 45.1 percent in 1988, and 43.0 percent in 1991. This decline excludes the rapidly expanded demand for cooked-food retailing during these years. Department stores' market share grew from 5.0 percent in 1962 to 13.3 percent, and grocery stores expanded from a mere 8.7 percent to 32.8 percent. The significance of grocery stores in the food-and-drink retail market has been further accentuated. (See Table 6.)

Amalgamation into Large Retail Enterprises

A retail company with a capital of ¥10 million or more and 50 or more employees is defined in Japan as a large retail enterprise. The total number of retail enterprises in 1991 was 1,294,532. Among these, large enterprises in terms of capital totaled 44,576 (3.4 percent), and in number of employees 8,592 (0.7 percent). The share of sales by large enterprises in terms of capital in 1991 was 53.4 percent, and in workforce 47.8 percent. Considering that these figures were 30.6 percent and 31.2 percent in 1972, respectively, the degree of amalgamation into large enterprises has been accelerated.

When examination was made of the organizational form of large enterprises having 50 or more employees, just 12.5 percent pursued a single-store business. Most enterprises conducted multistore operations, and companies having ten or more stores held a 34.7 percent market share. When judged by capital scale, large enterprises running a single-store business comprised the majority with 58.3 percent (Table 7).

As stated above, although many petty and occupational retail stores still remain in Japan, the declining tendency has been accelerated in the number of food-and-drink retail stores that present such characteristics as pettiness and an occupational nature. Similarity in retail structure to other advanced countries is forecast to grow in the future.

TABLE 6. Sales Share by Business Form

(%)

Year	1962	1972	1982	1985	1988	1991
Fabrics, clothing, personal articles	100.0	100.0	100.0	100.0	100.0	100.0
Department stores	23.8	27.3	33.5	34.1	34.5	35.2
Limited-assortment stores	72.9	68.1	61.4	60.3	60.2	59.6
Other	3.2	4.6	5.1	5.6	5.3	5.2
Food-and-drink merchandise	100.0	100.0	100.0	100.0	100.0	100.0
Department stores	5.0	7.7	12.6	12.8	12.6	13.3
Grocery stores	8.7	20.0	30.0	33.0	33.0	32.8
Limited-assortment stores	84.4	68.4	54.5	50.8	51.2	51.7
Other	1.9	3.9	2.9	3.4	3.2	2.2

(Material) Census of Commerce Table

TABLE 7. Sales Share of Large-Scale Retail Enterprises

(%)

Year	1972	1979	1982	1985	1988	1991
Enterprise with capital of ¥10 million minimum (¥100 million minimum)	30.6	33.0	45.4	47.7	51.9	53.4
	13.4	16.5	23.8	25.0	28.2	29.9
Enterprise with 50 employees minimum	31.2	30.0	41.4	43.6	47.6	47.8
(1,000 employees minimum)	9.0	12.2	17.5	17.6	20.7	21.1

(Material) Census of Commerce Table

CHANGES IN THE RETAIL INDUSTRY OPENING AND CLOSURE STRUCTURE

The number of retail stores, and especially of petty stores, has shown a remarkably declining tendency in recent years and has achieved massive structural change. The retail industry has been traditionally described as an industry with a low entry barrier. This means that one can open such a business easily with small capital. But retailing also has a high closure rate. It has been said that the retail industry demonstrated the so-called opening-and-closure structure of "multitudinous debuts and exits" (e.g., Palamountain, 1955). In recent Japan, however, it must be noticed that the structure has been changing from this type to one of "infrequent debuts and multitudinous exits," as is demonstrated in the declining number of retail stores. In the following section, long-term changes seen in the opening-and-closure structure of retail outlets will be discussed.[5]

Changes in the Number of Store Closures

Before estimating the number of store closures, let us look at the declining tendencies demonstrated by outlets classified by the year of establishment. The results are listed in Table 8, although this contains a skewed value in the 1974 survey whereby the number of stores established before 1944 increased from the previous survey. The number of stores established in 1944 or before diminished to 59.9 percent between 1968 and 1991, for an annual average-rate-of-decline of 2.2 percent. Similarly, the annual average-rate-of-decline for shops established between 1945 and 1954 was 2.7 percent, and 2.8 percent between 1955 and 1964. For stores established between 1965 and 1974, the annual average-rate-of-decline between 1976 and 1991 was 3.6 percent; and for shops established between 1975 and 1984, 4.3 percent between 1985 and 1991. These results show that the class of outlets established in more recent years has demonstrated a higher declining rate. This confirms that there were many early closures because of rash business openings.

The decline tendencies of the following three periods will now be discussed. The first period is between 1968 and 1976, the second is between 1976 and 1985, and the third is between 1985 and 1991. In the first period, shops established in 1944 or earlier decreased to 95.0 percent of the 1968 total. Similarly, stores established between 1945 and 1954 were reduced to 86.9 percent, and those established between 1955 and 1964 to 75.4 percent. These results indicated that the stores' survival rate was higher for older establishments, a tendency prevailing throughout all three periods. This was because outlets established in the past had already, before the survey period, outlasted the stores that were obliged to shut down early as a result of imprudent establishment. The average declining rates per year in the period were 1.2 percent, 1.7 percent, and 3.5 percent, respectively.

During the second period, stores established in 1944 or earlier diminished to 79.2 percent (since 1968, 72.0 percent); those established between 1945 and 1954 to 76.0 percent (66.1 percent); and those between 1955 and 1964 to 83.6 percent (63 percent). Shops established between 1965 and 1974 recorded the lowest survival rate of 69.5 percent. The survival rate of stores established in most recent years was the lowest since the first period. The annual average rates of decline in the second period were 2.6 percent, 3.0 percent, 2.0 percent, and 4.0 percent, respectively. Stores established in 1944 or before and those established between 1945 and 1954 demonstrated higher declining rates than in the first period. Outlets established between 1955 and 1964 that recorded the highest declining rate in the first period showed a lower rate of diminution.

In the third period, stores established in 1944 or before decreased to 83.2 percent (59.9 percent since 1968); those established between 1945 and 1954 to 81.0 percent (53.5 percent); those between 1955 and 1964 to 81.9 percent (51.6 percent); those between 1965 and 1974 to 83.2 percent (57.8 percent since 1976); and those between 1975 and 1984 to 76.6 percent. Here stores established in more recent years also demonstrated the lowest survival rate, and the phenomenon of rash entry and early closure was confirmed. The annual average rates of decline in the third period were 3.0 percent, 3.5 percent, 3.3 percent, 3.0 percent, and 4.3 percent, respectively. Stores established between 1965 and 1974 that recorded the highest declining rate in the second period showed a lower declining rate. Stores established before 1965 presented a higher declining rate than in the second period, which seemed to reflect the aging syndrome.

I sought a simple average without considering the aging effect. This concerned the changes in declining rates that stores classified by year of establishment demonstrate with advancing years. According to this, I estimated that the simple average rate will be 3.8 percent after ten years (more accurately, in ten to 19 years, the same in the following); 2.6 percent after 20 years; 2.2 percent after 30 years; 3.0 percent after 40 years; and 2.8 percent 50 years. This clearly reveals that the changes in declining rates describe a cycle where after passing the first decade, the declining rate will decrease until after three decades. After four decades, the declining rate will again become higher. Retail outlets thus appear to experience a declining period resulting from imprudent entries–a stable period with an established business foundation (for about 20 years)–a declining period because of aging of the owner (about ten years)–and a stable period brought about by business succession.

TABLE 8. Number of Retail Stores by Year of Establishment and Rate of Decline

Year established / Year	Number of shops	– 1944	1945–1954	1955–1964	1965–1974	1975–1984
1968		403,620	372,198	435,951		
1970		391,388	345,821	406,751		
1972		381,197	332,392	372,109		
1974		383,355	329,825	348,568		
1976		366,927	323,524	328,705	513,315	
1979		328,219	286,588	304,422	442,234	
1982		313,356	278,131	292,952	411,231	
1985		290,588	245,855	274,691	356,826	442,925
1988		282,792	221,337	249,294	325,999	380,839
1991		241,840	199,145	225,038	296,733	339,399

Annual
average rate of
decline (%)

Year				
1970	1.5	3.6	3.4		
1972	1.3	2.0	4.4		
1974	–	0.4	3.2		
1976	2.2	1.0	2.9		
1979	3.6	4.0	2.5	4.8	
1982	1.5	1.0	1.3	2.4	
1985	2.5	4.0	2.1	4.6	
1988	0.9	3.4	3.2	3.0	4.9
1991	5.1	3.5	3.4	3.1	3.7

(Material) Prepared from Census of Commerce Table

51

Table 9 shows the changes in the number of store closures. In 1974 and 1976 the number of store closures was small, each with an annual average of fewer than 30,000 stores closing, for a shutdown rate of about 2 percent. The annual average of store closures was maintained at about between 45,000 and 50,000 establishments except for the aforementioned two survey years. If these figures can be taken as a standard, the shutdowns of more than 70,000 stores in 1985 when the number of shops plunged, and of about 60,000 stores in 1991, demonstrated that remarkably large-scale shutdowns occurred at these points. The especially large increase of store closures occurring in 1985[6], when the establishment of large retail stores was strictly controlled, suggests that these closures were not exacerbated by competitive pressures. The internal problems of petty retailers–such as the aging of owners and lack of successors–seem to have been major factors.

Changes in the Number of New Shops

As is clearly shown in Table 9, the annual average rate of new openings has been diminishing year after year. The number of new establishments decreased from 79,904 in 1970 to 42,733 in 1991. The opening rate decreased from 5.6 percent to 2.6 percent. This declining tendency of retail stores in Japan has been triggered by the increase in store closures and decrease in openings. When comparing the figure of 1991 with 1970's, the number of store closures increased 36.5 percent and store openings diminished 46.6 percent. This demonstrated that the decrease in store openings rather than the increase in store closures has become a larger factor in the decrease in the number of retail outlets.

Among retail shops with one or two employees and food-and-drink retail stores that diminished remarkably in number, store openings were reduced by half. The decrease in the debut of these stores is tied to the reduction in the number of store openings as a whole. It is obvious that the characteristic is fading whereby in retailing one can open a shop with small capital, or that other conditions of openings in the retail markets are changing. If regional oligopoly is brought about and consumers' interests are harmed through establishment of a retail-structural type of infrequent debuts and multitudinous exits in a country with relatively high land prices such as Japan, a government distribution policy may be required that encourages the opening of retail stores.

CONCLUSION

This analysis clarifies the fact that Japan's retail structure is experiencing a great transitional period. Through a substantial reduction in the

TABLE 9. Changes in Number of Store Openings and Closures

(Shop, %)

	Store closures		Store openings	
	Average number of closures	Average closure rate	Average number of store openings	Average opening rate
1970	44,090	3.2	79,904	5.6
1972	52,314	3.7	76,820	5.2
1974	29,594	2.0	66,218	4.4
1976	29,997	2.0	70,663	4.6
1979	46,026	3.0	72,640	4.5
1982	45,040	2.8	69,839	4.2
1985	74,530	4.5	51,701	3.0
1988	49,650	3.2	52,242	3.2
1991	60,196	3.9	42,733	2.6

(Material) Census of Commerce Table

number of petty stores and food-and-drink outlets, Japan's retail structure has become similar to other developed countries'. Along with the changes in the opening and closing structure from the "multitudinous debuts and exits" type to the "infrequent debuts and multitudinous exits" type, this tendency will continue to accelerate.

Notice must also be taken of the fact that the aforementioned factors that prescribe the distribution system in Japan are also changing in quality. The average growth rate of the retail market fell from 14.5 percent in the seventies to 5.1 percent in the eighties. The market expansion that has supported the existence of many petty retailers can no longer be relied upon. Our domestic organizations' traditional business practices and vertical relationships have been pressured to change so that a more streamlined system will be reconstructed through the growth of networks. Among chain stores that were quick to develop an information network, enterprises have appeared that constructed a more efficient business organization and operational system. An increase in suburban consumers has made automotive shopping excursions a routine matter. The social advancement of housewives has lessened the number of shop visits. The revised Large-Scale Retail Store Law of 1992 has intensified competition over space and among large retail stores. This should exert considerable indirect influence upon small and medium retail establishments. It can thus be concluded that changes in the initial conditions that prescribed the distribution system in Japan have affected the opening and closure structure of retail outlets and are encouraging reforms in the retail structure.

The distribution system, because it is amenable to strong geographical, social, and cultural influences in the country where it operates, cannot always be structured according to a universal model (Tajima, 1989). In structural aspects–specifically, the declining importance of the traditional distribution system–our distribution system may be quite similar to those of other advanced countries. I did not touch upon the wholesale industry in this paper. I only wish to indicate that the number of wholesale steps is not as multitudinous as conventionally believed (Nariu and Flath, 1993; Kakeda, 1993); and that it seems possible that an efficient system of large wholesalers and a partnership-type organization different from the conventional "keiretsu" or "cho-ai" systems will become dominant.

NOTES

1. Since the 1988 survey, the following retail establishments not included up to that point have become survey subjects:

(1) establishments which are in the government office, the schools, enterprises, etc., and are managed by other bodies.

(2) establishments which sell goods by visiting sales or mail order and do not have sales space.

At present, however, (stalls and street vendors) and (stands and booths in buildings that vend tickets for events such as movies or baseball games) are not included in the survey. Data for 1988 and 1991 in this analysis indicated results based on the new survey subjects. The number of retail stores newly added as survey subjects in 1988 was 12,351.

2. According to the Census of Commerce, regularly paid family members are defined as regular employees. It is assumed, therefore, that unincorporated establishments without regular employees are extremely occupational.

3. Vegetable and fruit stores, meat and poultry stores, and fresh-fish stores are included in fresh food stores. Manufacturing-retail food stores include confectionery and bakery stores, manufacturing-retail processed-food stores, and delicatessens. Food-and-drink retail outlets excluding the above retailers and grocers are called other food stores.

4. General-merchandise outlets having 50 or more employees are included with department stores.

5. The following is how store openings and entry rates are calculated in this paper. Taking the year 1991 as an example, the difference in the number of establishments founded before 1987 and included in the 1988 survey, and the total number of stores as of 1991, is the number of store openings that were established during the period. The entry rate is the value obtained from dividing the number of store openings by the total number of stores in 1988, and adjusting the result to the annual average. The calculation method for store closures and the withdrawal rate is as follows. With 1991 as an example, the difference in the number of stores established before 1987 and included in the 1991 survey, and the number of shops established before 1987 and included in the 1988 survey, is the number of store closures that occurred during the period. The withdrawal rate is the value obtained from dividing the number of store closures of 1988 by that of 1991, and adjusting the result to the annual average.

6. During the period, the establishment of large retail stores was in effect frozen by administrative guidance from the Ministry of International Trade and Industry. This was in addition to restrictions prescribed by the Large-Scale Retail Store Law.

REFERENCES

Arakawa, Y. (1962), Kourishogyokozoron (The Theory of Retailing System), (Chikura Shobou).
Czinkota, M. R. (1985), "Distribution in Japan: Problems and Changes," Columbia Journal of World Business (Fall), 65-71.
_____ and J. Woronoff (1986), Japan's Market: The Distribution System (Praeger Publishers).
Goldman, A. (1991), "Japan's Distribution System: Institutional Structure, In-

ternal Political Economy, and Modernization," *Journal of Retailing, 67* (Summer), 154-183.

_____ (1992), "Evaluating the Performance of the Japanese Distribution System," *Journal of Retailing, 68* (Spring), 11-39.

Hayashi, S. (1964), Ryutsukakumei (Revolution of Distribution), (Chuoukouronsha).

Kakeda, Y. (1992), "Ryutsu channel soshiki no henka to tenbo" (Revolution of Distribution Channel) *Japan Marketing Journal, 44,* 14-21.

_____ (1993), "Shogyotokei ni yoru wagakuni ryutsugyo no kozobunseki" Wagakuni ryutsu no genkyo to kadai (The Analysis of Japan's Distribution System, The Contemporary Issue of Japanese Distribution System), Y. Tajima, ed. (Japan Productivity Center).

Manifold, D. L. (1993), "Accessing Japan's Distribution Channels," in The Japanese Distribution System, Michael R. Czinkota and Masaaki Kotabe, ed. (Probus Publishing Company).

Nariu, T. and D. Flath (1993), "The Complexity of Wholesale Distribution Channels in Japan," in The Japanese Distribution System, M. R. Czinkota and M. Kotabe, ed. (Probus Publishing Company).

Palamountain, J. C., Jr. (1955), The Politics of Distribution, (Harvard University Press).

Satoh, H. (1971), Nihon no ryutsukozo (The Japan's Distribution System) (Yuuhikaku).

Sharma, A. and L. V. Dominguez (1992), "Channel Evolution: A Framework for Analysis," *Journal of the Academy of Marketing Science, 20* (Winter), 1-15.

Shimaguchi, M. (1977), Marketing Channels in Japan (University of Michigan Research Press).

_____ and W. Lazer (1979), "Japanese Distribution Channels: Invisible Barriers to Market Entry," MSU Business Topics (Winter), 49-62.

Suzuki, Y. and A. Yamanaka (1962), "Tokyo-to ni okeru kourigyo no tenkai" (The Revolution of Retailing in Tokyo) Shogyo no tenkai to mondai (The Changes and Problems of Commerce) F. Muramoto, ed. (Yuuhikaku).

_____ (1993), "Large-Scale Retail Law: Historical Background and Social Implications," in The Japanese Distribution System, M. R. Czinkota and M. Kotabe, ed. (Probus Publishing Company).

Tajima, Y. (1989), "Hikaku ryutsuron(5)" (The Theory of Comparative Distribution System) *The Journal of Marketing and Distribution* (May), 14-18.

Tamura, M. (1986), Nihongata ryutsu system (The Japan's Distribution System), (Chikura Shobou).

Three Methods to Deal with the Uncertain Market Environment: Establishing New Intrachannel Relationships

Takeshi Moriguchi

SUMMARY. In dealing with the present uncertain market environment three principal measures are being taken: micromarketing, the strategic use of information systems, and strategic alliances. Each is closely involved in the new intrachannel relationship that is the change from competition to cooperation.

This paper outlines these three methods and introduces the MID (Marketing Intelligence Development organization), a joint R&D group of manufacturers, wholesalers, and retailers, as an example of intrachannel cooperation in Japan.

INTRODUCTION

Uncertainty is increasing in the Japanese markets as a result of the present unstable economic conditions brought about by the recent collapse of the bubble economy and the subsequent recession. To deal with this uncertainty, companies are taking vigorous measures, concentrating upon restructuring.

Takeshi Moriguchi is Chief Researcher for The Distribution Economics Institute of Japan. He holds an MBA from the Graduate School of Systems Management, Tsukuba University.

[Haworth co-indexing entry note]: "Three Methods to Deal with the Uncertain Market Environment: Establishing New Intrachannel Relationships." Moriguchi, Takeshi. Co-published simultaneously in the *Journal of Marketing Channels* (The Haworth Press, Inc.) Vol. 3, No. 3, 1994, pp. 57-69; and: *Japanese Distribution Channels* (ed: Takeshi Kikuchi) The Haworth Press, Inc., 1994, pp. 57-69. Multiple copies of this article/chapter may be purchased from The Haworth Document Delivery Center [1-800-3-HAWORTH; 9:00 a.m. - 5:00 p.m. (EST)].

This paper discusses three principal marketing measures: micromarketing, the strategic use of information systems, and strategic alliances. Each has been a recent major marketing topic. Common points can be seen in these three measures although they appear superficially to be completely different. First, each measure is closely related to the scanner data that have caused a great change in recent marketing. These data are a key concept in changing the intrachannel relationship, primarily by scanner-data sharing. An example of the strategic use of information systems is the establishment of channels that are managed by information systems. Another point is that an important feature in the trend from mass-marketing to micro-marketing is individual-channel marketing. Strategic alliances between manufacturers and distributors are a final goal of that trend.

This paper will outline these three concepts and will introduce the MID. This is an R&D group including manufacturers, wholesalers, and retailers organized and operated in Japan in light of the three concepts.

GROWING MARKET UNCERTAINTY

The market environment is changing rapidly, adding to market uncertainty. Among the factors of market uncertainty, two are commonly discussed by researchers. One is the complexity or heterogeneity of the market. The other is market instability or its dynamics.

These two factors are expanding recently because of several causes. First, the increased diversification in consumption is incrementing the complexity or heterogeneity of the market environment. Most of the individual markets are now difficult to view as homogeneous entities but must be grasped as a collection of different segments. This directly affects the increase of market heterogeneity and complexity. Ongoing internationalization and diversification of business activities also contribute to these growing market characteristics. Market heterogeneity and complexity are unavoidably added when businesses' markets expand.

Second, the quicker changes in consumers' preferences, and products' resulting shorter life cycles, are making the market more unstable and more dynamic. Continuously accelerated technological innovation also contributes to the instability and dynamics. As typified by the computer market, especially that of word processors, change becomes a fixed state in the market because of the constant acceleration of technological innovations. The closer relationship between politics and the economy is also an important aspect for the market environment nowadays. Trade frictions or deregulation policies may give rise to drastic market structural changes.

One of the more important points is that companies' countermeasures to such market-environment uncertainty can exacerbate the uncertainty. Facing the increasing uncertainty of a market, most companies probably adopt a strategy of business diversification to distribute risk and to try to find another channel for growth. This, too, can increase market uncertainty. Business diversification and corporate internationalization can intensify competition in markets, giving rise to more instability and uncertainty. Another point is that with intensified competition and diversification of consumption, companies' measures including product differentiation and market fragmentation are likely to increase consumption diversification and the shortening of product life cycles. Companies' countermeasures to combat market uncertainty can thus produce further uncertainty. Accordingly, businesses should recognize that uncertainty is a constant factor that must be taken into account in the market environment.

A MEASURE TO COUNTER MARKET UNCERTAINTY: MICRO-MARKETING

One of the measures to counter today's market uncertainty is to view a market on a microbasis. It is inefficient to view a complex and heterogeneous market as a whole and to apply the same marketing method to the entire market. It is also ineffective to take the same marketing measures without long-run changes for a dynamic and unstable market. There therefore exists a major trend from mass-marketing toward micro-marketing.

Micro-marketing means markets in a specific place at a specific time. Nonaka (1974) has presented the previously-mentioned two dimensions of market uncertainty as diversity in time and space. In response to this, micro-marketing is an attempt to capture a market of specific time and space so as to reduce the environmental uncertainty. Accordingly, data used for such marketing must be gathered in terms of specified time and space. Companies do not have data in this mode at present. Their existing data are independent of time and space in the market because their data are for mass marketing. For example, manufacturers have the marketing data for their total sales-promotion budget by brands. Manufacturers, however, have no data on budgetary translation into the when, where, and what of promotion activities. The sales data preserved by manufacturers usually concerns shipment, but does not represent actual consumer demand. The existing data of actual demand such as diary panel data and home-scan panel data that is recently replacing it, is aimed at representing the whole market but not specific time and space in the market.

The data gathered so far thus represents consumers' behavior and the company's activities, both on an average basis for perusal regarding the correlation between them. Correlation between averages, however, is nearly meaningless in today's increasingly uncertain market environment. To find the cause and effect relationship between a company's actions and consumer responses, it is necessary first to specify market time and space. For instance, to be observed is marketing activity in a specific store at a specific time and the consumers' response, or a stimulus to specific consumers and their response. Scanner data is most effective to observe this relationship.

The advantages of scanner data are easy integration and continuity–besides the elaborateness, celerity, and precision that have often been mentioned. Scanner data are continuous and can be easily integrated with other related data. The scanner data show sales results, and can help to find out the cause and effect relationship between the company's actions and sales results only if integrated with data on the causes. Such integration can be easily performed because the scanner data concern a specific store at a specific time, or the data with specific spaces and times that are used as common keys of reference.

Uncertainty in the market is thus becoming constant; micro-marketing is regarded as an important measure in this regard; and scanner data is increasingly vital for use in micro-marketing.

A MEASURE TO COUNTER MARKET UNCERTAINTY: INFORMATION-SYSTEM ADAPTATION TO THE ENVIRONMENT

Management strategy and organization have been discussed conceptually or on a substantive basis as factors that directly affect business results. A management information system, however, must be added to these as equally important. This is clearly seen in the frequency of discussion regarding SIS (Strategic Information Systems). Furthermore, we must now consider the expansion of information systems: not merely within a company, but more broadly in a vertical-channel system in some cases as discussed subsequently. Information systems are thus being taken as the primary weapons for intrachannel system competition.

Against this background, this Section will try to visualize the role of information systems in adapting to today's uncertain market environment.

The essential matter of management in this uncertain environment is effective adaptation. Theories concerning organizational adaptation to the environment are generally called contingency theories. These address this matter in terms of the scope of information processing and the unit that performs it. A study by Burns and Stalker (1961) concluded that an organic type of organization was more effective in an unstable environment, while a mechanical type of organization was superior in a stable environment. According to Galbraith (1972), the matter of adaptation to environmental uncertainty could resolve itself into the reduction of a company's information-processing load and the increase of information-processing capacity.

Such discussions have been made mainly in the field of organizational theories. This means that they have been considered to be concerned primarily with organizational design or interaction between management organization and strategy. Conversely, in this paper, the information system is treated as a factor that is separate from and has the same importance as strategy and organization. The first reason for this is that support for an information system is essential for managerial decision-making amid an uncertain environment because of the large volume of necessary data and the requisite rapidity of decision-making. The second reason is that there exist cases where the interaction among management strategy, management organization, and an information system is utilized for adaptation to the environment. This new role of information systems is now recognized in the SIS sphere.

Discussed in the following Subsections will be two aspects of the working of information systems in adaptation to the environment. One of these is adaptation by adjustment with information systems. The other is adaptation by creation, utilizing information systems.

Adaptation by Adjustment: MDSS

The heterogeneity and complexity of the uncertain market environment enormously increase the volume of data to be processed. At the same time, the instability and dynamics of the environment make necessary frequent changes and modifications in plans. Quick feedback of business results is necessary, and plans should be immediately changed according to the feedback if necessary. The capability to perceive and respond quickly to changes is required, rather than intricately detailed plans. Accordingly, a necessity is the repeated feedback of business results into planning. The mechanism to execute rapid feedback is vitally important.

The support of information systems is therefore essential for information processing and for decision-making organizations to deal with the uncertainty of the environment. The DSS (Decision Support System) is an information system that provides support for decision making.

Morton (1971) created this concept. He devised a framework for information systems by combining Anthony's (1965) and Simon's (1960) classifications of decisions. Then Gorry and Morton (1971) put forth the DSS to be utilized for decision making on semistructural management matters (1971). They suggested that semistructural problems could not be solved by any single member of the decision-making group and the information system. Gorry and Morton thus proposed the DSS, a man-machine-system. Besides DSS, similar concepts such as the ESS (Executive Support System), MSS (Management Support System), and EIS (Executive Information System) have been brought forward. The support of information systems for decision making is thus regarded as important.

With increasing uncertainty in the market environment, nonstructural and semistructural matters are given more weight in marketing decisions. Accordingly, the MDSS (marketing decision support system), which is the DSS for marketing decisions, becomes much more vital.

An MDSS can be the information system that makes possible adaptation by adjustment to the unstable market environment. To use MDSS for that purpose the following conditions should be satisfied.

- Information systems are required to be capable of solving problems step-by-step: such as by using simulation models rather than optimization models. This is because decisions should be made rapidly and because they deal with nonstructural and semistructural problems.
- For the above reason, decision-makers themselves should handle the systems.
- Accordingly, decision-makers must have the interface to permit end-user computing.
- Specialization and integration of organizations in a company are needed for effective adaptation to the uncertain environment. The systems therefore should be configured in conformity with specialized and integrated organizations. Preferable systems should actually have autonomous databases in specialized organizations and integrate them into the whole-company database.
- The models should be adaptable to environmental changes.

In summary, the MDSS should enable marketing decision-makers to make decisions on a trial-and-error basis.

Adaptation by Creation: SIS

MDSS systems exert considerable power in adapting to the market environment by adjustment. Quite a few people, however, point out that adapting by creation, or the ability to create change, becomes more useful than adapting by adjustment inasmuch as the market environment changes faster. This Subsection will discuss the role of information systems in adapting by creation.

SIS, the concept promoted by Wiseman (1985), represents the concepts of adaptation to the environment by creation with information systems. SIS are generally constructed to gain and maintain competitive advantage. Accordingly, the construction of an SIS itself is part of a company's competitive strategy. An SIS can also be regarded as part of business-diversification strategy as seen in successful cases where companies expanded their business areas subsequent to the construction of systems.

Most of the SIS organize by means of networks. They expand the information-processing capability of their own network that includes outside organizations. SIS organize by an expansion of capability. Companies with SIS gain competitive advantage with the interactive process of a network's information processing ability and the expansion of the network. It can thus be understood that the SIS assists in adaptation to the environment through an organic relationship between strategy, organization, and an information system. Inasmuch as environmental uncertainty grows to a high degree, consideration should be given to the expansion of information processing at the level of a vertical-channel system rather than at that of a single company. Accordingly, future considerations regarding companies' information systems are (a) how a channel system can ensure a competitive advantage over other channels by expanding the system's information-processing ability, and (b) how a company can simultaneously assume leadership in the channel system.

One of the conditions for successfully solving these is that an information system be adaptable. An example of such a system is Seven Eleven Japan's information system with its core scanning system called EOS (Electronic Ordering System). This has evolved with frequent modifications since its introduction. Replacements in this system have easily been implemented because the cost of the system is borne by the company headquarters. With replacements, the system is adaptable to environmental changes. The system enables the headquarters to maintain its leadership over the franchisees and to have a competitive edge over rival chain stores. This would never be the case if they imposed upon the franchisees the cost of system replacement.

Dealing with Marketing Environmental Uncertainty: Strategic Alliances

Change has occurred since the late eighties in the recognition of marketing channels, along with the emerging channel systems constructed with the core of an information system as mentioned previously. The change is that the friendly relationship between seller and purchaser is increasingly emphasized in recognition of dealing. This was previously considered to be a mutually antagonistic relationship. Intrachannel dealing is now beginning to be regarded as a win-win game where both the purchaser and the seller gain, rather than a zero-sum game.

An example of win-win games is the strategic cooperation between P&G (Proctor and Gamble Inc.) and Wal-Mart which began in the late eighties. According to the late Sam Walton, a major step toward this cooperation was the sharing of computer information (Walton and Huey, 1992).

ECR (Efficient Consumer Response), proposed by the FMI (Food Marketing Institute) in 1993, is based on a similar idea. FMI is a plan to try to reduce 41% of inventories and to save $30 billion of operational costs of the nation's stores by means of a comprehensive review of the distribution system from upstream to downstream. This will be done with the effective use of scanner data by manufacturers and distributors. The plan has the final goal of reducing the consumer prices of grocery and sundries by 11% on average. The sharing of information is essential to the implementation of this ECR plan. It will become possible to make overall distribution more efficient by makers' and distributors' mutual sharing of inventory, sales, and shipment information.

The concern now is how to improve the productivity of overall distribution. Cooperation, co-marketing, and co-merchandising between manufacturers and distributors are thus required.

INTRODUCTION OF MID

Keeping in mind the above three methods that are regarded as important for adaptation to the uncertain market environment, this Section will introduce an R&D organization in Japan called MID (Marketing Intelligence Development organization).

MID Characteristics

MID was organized by the DEI (The Distribution Economics Institute of Japan). It is a joint-study organization with the participation of consumer-goods makers, computer makers, retailers, and wholesalers. It is a rare organization globally in that rival companies in a business are mutually engaged in research and development. The number of its participating companies in the summer of 1993 was 39.

One of the major themes of MID is the effective utilization of scanner data for marketing and merchandising. A unique characteristic of this organization is that it does not pursue broad data, but rather deep data. In this regard the organization is different from other data-service entities. MID pays little attention to data representing the market. Instead, MID focuses upon a variety of data to grasp cause and effect relationships between marketing factors and sales.

MID actually gathers scanner data, so-called causal data that comprise sales-factor data in stores, so-called scan-panel data that includes consumers' purchasing histories, etc. Causal data items are shown in Table 1. As seen in Table 1, MID collects and provides with photographs of shelf display and special display by on-line network. Member companies can review or evaluate the sales of goods with visual images of the displays.

MID has selected 16 stores throughout Japan for survey and experimentation. It collects scanner data from all of them, and causal data from 14. These stores have a closed business area where there are fewer competitors, because the data of such a store can more clearly reflect sales results caused by selling factors.

Scanner-panel data on 14,000 households are collected at half of the 16 survey and experimentation stores. The above-mentioned condition of the stores allows MID to capture most of the purchases of the panelists. Accordingly, the cause and effect between marketing measures and sales results are quite precisely known because detailed analysis can be made of the relationship between sales and contributing marketing factors at specific stores.

MID does not pursue representation of the market, but rather the cause and effect relationship between sales and marketing factors because of increasing market uncertainty. As mentioned above, there is minimal significance in looking over a market as a whole when the market is enormously diversified in terms of time and space. MID, therefore, specifies time and space that can be keys to integrate a variety of data of cause and effect. MID pays much more attention to this integration.

MID also emphasizes the sharing of data. Retailers, wholesalers, and manufacturers can discuss merchandising at specific stores on a common ground by sharing data on outlets. MID is engaged in R&D activities on different themes based on such shared data. Its major themes are the development of scanner-data-analysis methods, study of consumers' purchasing behavior in stores, etc. These are of common interest for all member companies so that the themes are developed as common concerns. Conversely, the development of marketing know-how concerning a specific product category is conducted by the companies involved. They have meetings and do joint R&D on how to increase productivities.

The R&D methods comprise not only the analysis of observed data that

TABLE 1. Causal Data Items Collected by MID

- Special displays
- Volumes of displayed products at special displays
- Location of special displays
- Premiums
- Bundle sales
- Demonstration sales
- Coupons
- Features
- Location of shelves
- Number of faces of each product
- Weather
- Temperature
- Photos of special displays
- Photos of shelf displays
- Floor-layout drawing

serve to grasp daily changes in marketing factors–employing causal data and its effect with scanner data and scan panel data–but also experiments in stores to examine the effect of measures by experimentally controlling sales factors. Accordingly, this organization is regarded not just as a data-collecting and service system to observe the market, but as a marketing-testing system.

In MID, companies are jointly engaged in R&D activities concerning marketing or merchandising. This is a realization of co-marketing and co-merchandising.

MID's Data-Analysis System (Marketer's Desk)

MID's host computer is connected with its member companies through a work-station network. Member companies can retrieve on-line the above-mentioned information including photos. The scanner-data-analysis system called the Marketer's Desk that is used through workstations is also provided for member companies. Its characteristics are as follows.

–Provision of raw data

The Marketer's Desk provides raw data that users can aggregate or process in any grouping. Total values about the market are hardly useful for micro-marketing. It is essential to be able to regroup data at users' discretion to aggregate or reprocess for micro-marketing. The maintenance and provision of raw data enable users to do this.

–Provision of data on all products

Scanner data, causal data, and scan-panel data on all the subject products (food and sundries) in the survey stores are available to member companies. Member companies can be aware not only of data regarding their own categories of products, but also of the total-sales trend at outlets.

–End-user computing function

MID's computer is equipped with spread-sheet software capable of linkup with databases. Users can use this software to retrieve and process data. This end-user computing function is a strong feature of the MID system.

–Model-analysis function

The volume of scanner data is so enormous that it is difficult to obtain meaningful information from the raw data provided. Marketing models are very useful for users to obtain pertinent information from the raw data.

MID provides marketing models ranging from a primitive one that calculates and outputs a graph of the price elasticity of a specific product–illustrating price changes and corresponding sales–to a sophisticated model that calculates P/L by product category.

–Use of GUI (Graphical User Interface)

The Marketer's Desk is operated wholly through GUI. Marketing decision-makers are not computer experts but specialists in marketing. For this reason, GUI has been adopted. It enables users to handle the system easily by moving a mouse around switches on the display rather than via keyboard operation.

This system at present deals only with the data of MID's survey and experimentation stores. Its future expansion, however, into an intracompany information system with the core of the MID system, is contemplated. Two directions in such expansion would be considered. One could be the construction of an MDSS with the core of the Marketer's Desk. Member companies, of course, have their own marketing data. They must construct an information system to retrieve and process data such as their shipment data and syndicate data purchased from research institutions on an integrated basis. The MID considers that it is a role of the Marketer's Desk to provide a prototype of the MDSS with an integrated database.

Another direction could be the expansion of the present system into an SIS. Through the Marketer's Desk, scanner data is shared by manufacturers, wholesalers, and retailers. An information network to strive to make the entire distribution more efficient by sharing data could be constructed in the future.

To realize this, the sharing of data on a much more extended basis, not just on a limited number of stores, would be necessary. The Marketer's Desk is contemplated as a base system for such an information network.

CONCLUSION

One of the present major concerns is how a channel system as a whole can improve its productivity. One of the effective measures is a strategic alliance between manufacturers and distributors. A key concept for the improvement of productivity of an overall channel system is the sharing of data, and the shared data would mainly be scanner data.

Japanese companies are unfortunately more reluctant to disclose their own data to other companies than are U.S. companies. This is one of the reasons why there exist no large scanner-data-service institutions. Some manufacturers and retailers, however, have begun joint product development with their scanner data. In the future there will be cooperation between companies not only in product development but in all areas of marketing. We hope to promote the sharing of data for the establishment of a new intrachannel relationship.

REFERENCES

Anthony, R. N. (1965), "Planning and Control System," Harvard University.
Burns, T. and Stalker, G. M. (1961), The Management of Innovation, Tavistock.
Galbraith, J. R. (1972), Designing Complex Organizations, Addison Wesley.
Gorry, G. A. and Morton, S. (1971), "A Framework for a Management Information System," Sloan Management Review, Fall.

Morton M. S. S. (1971), "Management Decision-Support Systems: Computer-Based Support for Decision-Making," Harvard University, Graduate School of Business Administration.

Nonaka, I. (1974), Soshiki to Shijo (Organization and Market) Chikurashobo (in Japanese).

Simon, H. A. (1960), "The New Science of Management Decision," Prentice-Hall.

Walton, S. and Huey, J. (1992), Sam Walton, Made in America: My Story, Doubleday.

Wiseman, C. (1985), "Strategy and Computers: Information Systems as Competitive Weapons," Dow Jones-Irwin.

Some Characteristics
of Business Practices
in Japan

Toshiaki Taga
Yukihiko Uehara

SUMMARY. The purpose of this paper is, first, to describe those business practices which are peculiar to the Japanese distribution system, and second, to attempt to provide a rationale for them. The transaction system in Japan has some characteristics, which may seem more or less different from those in other developed countries, such as choosing business partners based on the amount of past and previous transactions, various and diverse transaction terms, and long-term transactional relations. In this paper, we clarify that these characteristics are based upon Japanese emphasis on the importance of mutual trust relationships, and these keep transaction costs low.

INTRODUCTION

Motivation of Study

There have been a number of studies of the Japanese distribution system, especially in the 1980s.[1] Most of these have focused analysis on the structural aspect of the distribution system. These studies point out several facts, based on statistical analysis, such as:

Toshiaki Taga is Director, U.S.-Japan Institute, 3624 Market Street, Philadelphia, PA 19104. Yukihiko Uehara is Professor of Marketing at Meijigakuin University, 1-2-37 Shiroganedai, Minato, Tokyo 108, Japan.

[Haworth co-indexing entry note]: "Some Characteristics of Business Practices in Japan." Taga, Toshiaki, and Yukihiko Uehara. Co-published simultaneously in the *Journal of Marketing Channels* (The Haworth Press, Inc.) Vol. 3, No. 3, 1994, pp. 71-89; and: *Japanese Distribution Channels* (ed: Takeshi Kikuchi) The Haworth Press, Inc., 1994, pp. 71-89. Multiple copies of this article/chapter may be purchased from The Haworth Document Delivery Center [1-800-3-HAWORTH; 9:00 a.m. - 5:00 p.m. (EST)].

Compared with the U.S. and Europe,

1. The number of business establishments in distribution in Japan is quite large, and their size tends to be small.
2. Distribution channels in Japan are multi-layered.
3. Manufacturers in Japan tend to have stronger control and power over their distribution channels.

In most of these studies, the aspect of actual transactions has been pretty much neglected, or at best been briefly touched upon.[2] In general terms, previous studies focused primarily on analysis of the system structure, and paid secondary attention to the aspect of action and processes in the system. Both parts, structure and process, are required of researchers to come to a better understanding of the whole system of distribution in Japan.

The purpose of our study on business practices is to complement previous studies by focusing directly on the aspect of behavior and processes, and to provide the first important step toward a proper understanding of how the distribution system works in Japan.

In order to achieve the above stated objective we have conducted field studies on actual business practices in Japan.[3] We have made special efforts to obtain qualitative rather than quantitative data. As to the approach, we decided not to resort to the method of a pre-determined survey-questionnaire. Rather, we decided to interview a few dozen businessmen in charge of buying and selling at different stages of distribution channels of the products we specified. In our judgement, this method, at this early stage of research, was considered best for obtaining "facts" about action and processes in the system of transactions. The explanation of transactional practices in this paper is based on the analysis of the facts obtained through these interviews.

Scope and Viewpoint of Analysis

First, the specific types of transaction practices in Japan differ from product to product. The question arises as to which group of products should be the target for our analysis. We decided to choose those out of the "highly representative groups of products." By "highly representative groups of products," we refer to those groups of products which share most of the general characteristics found in the current business transactions in Japan. The groups of merchandise subject to the following situation, for example, are considered to be lacking a high degree of representation:

1. tight government control,
2. in existence for a long time, but traded only in a traditional, old-fashioned way,
3. relatively small demand,
4. traded rather infrequently, and
5. came into being in recent days, and are newly emerged so that common practices have not been established.

One good example of a highly representative group is processed foods. In this paper, whenever an actual example is needed to make the description of a particular practice more concrete, there is a focus on the distribution of processed foods. Of course, that part of practices relevant to groups of merchandise other than processed foods will be treated within the scope of our analysis.

Secondly, there is a question of the viewpoint from which to sift the collected data in order to summarize, integrate and analyze them. To clearly differentiate one system of transaction practices from another, we need to look at the separate dimensions of an aspect of a transaction. Four such dimensions can be considered here.[4]

A. Formation of the Parties to the Transaction
   What qualifications are required for any body to become a party to a particular transaction? What characteristics can be depicted in the formation of the parties involved?
B. Arrangement of Terms and Conditions of Transactions
   What items are mentioned in the agreement, and what items are relatively important?
C. Formality of Transactions
   What part of transactions are considered formal? How important is the formality of transactions?
D. Continuity of Transactions
   How strong is the intention of both parties to continue the established transactional relationship?

These four dimensions we considered in summarizing and analyzing the data obtained in our study.

Thirdly, in this study, we attempted to focus on those parts of business practices that have been relatively stable and regular. Transaction behavior changes depending on a particular competition pattern, a kind of dispute along a specified distribution channel, and the way these disputes get resolved. These matters are outside the scope of the study at this point.

SOME CHARACTERISTICS OF FORMATION
OF THE TRANSACTION PARTIES IN JAPAN

The Theme/Analysis

Some of the characteristics of the formation of negotiating parties in Japanese business will be analyzed from the perspective of qualifications—that is, how the parties involved in a transaction/negotiation are screened beforehand. In principle, if all other conditions are to be ignored, a party would be considered "qualified" if it is interested in either purchasing or selling. But in practice, particularly in many industrialized societies, these "qualifications" are predetermined or pre-screened. For instance, a chocolate manufacturer will not sell chocolate directly to a consumer, since the consumer has been omitted from one of the qualified groups, which may purchase the chocolate, via pre-screening. The question is, what are the bases of such pre-screening?

In Japan, there are two bases for pre-screening. One is universally used in other industrialized countries, the other is unique to Japan. This analysis will focus on these two bases.

Qualification for Transaction Parties with Respect to "Order Quantity Criterion"

In order to pre-screen those eligible to participate in the transaction, the "Order Quantity Criterion" is used. This criterion implies that someone who wishes to establish his status as a buyer of a particular product must constantly be able to place at least the minimum order quantity set by the seller of the said product. The buyer will be picked from among those who satisfy this criterion.

The "Order Quantity Criterion" is determined by the seller in order to screen those buyers with whom he wishes to do business. The individual sellers, depending upon their strategy, decide upon the quantity level.

With regard to this criterion, one must observe the following facts. First, it can be said that the "Order Quantity Criterion" is set according to some socially meaningful functions at each stage of distribution channels (which might be called the "Principle of Correspondence to Distribution Functions"). For example, as products, such as processed foods, move along toward the end of the channel, the small quantity-multiple item type assortment function is required. In correspondence with this requirement, as one moves toward the end of distribution, the standard order level of the "Order Quantity Criterion" gets lower. In the transaction between a retailer and a household consumer, the standard order level, except for special cases, declines to zero, so that any household consumer will end up becoming qualified to be a trading partner of the retailer.

Secondly, in a modern, industrialized society, the "Openness-Nondiscrimination Principle" is called for in the application of the "Order Quantity Criterion." In advanced, industrialized countries, there seems to be the following consensus in applying the criterion:

1. A seller must be able to make the "Order Quantity Criterion" open and public. That is, whoever wishes to transact with the seller must be in a situation in which he can get to know beforehand the details about the "Order Quantity Criterion."
2. A seller is not allowed to change the "Order Quantity Criterion" for a particular product from buyer to buyer. That is, a seller cannot discriminate between buyer X and buyer Y when applying the "Order Quantity Criterion."

For example, suppose a retailer is unable to deal directly with a manufacturer, and can only place an order through a wholesaler. This may be accounted for by the fact that the retailer can satisfy the wholesaler's "Order Quantity Criterion," but not the manufacturer's ("The Principle of Correspondence to Distribution Functions"). If and when the retailer expands his business to the point where he can meet the manufacturer's "Order Quantity Criterion," then he becomes qualified to deal directly with the manufacturer, as well as the wholesaler ("The Principle of Openness-Nondiscrimination").

In Japan, the "Order Quantity Criterion" is practiced to determine whether or not a party is qualified to participate in business transactions. We must mention another identifiable criterion which keeps the "Order Quantity Criterion" from being fully effective.

Qualifications for a Business Partner with Respect to "Continuity of Transactions Criterion"

In addition to the "Order Quantity Criterion," we can identify the "Continuity of Transactions Criterion" as a criterion for screening those who may be eligible to engage in transactions. In Japan, one must notice that the latter criterion works to constrain the full application of the former.

The "Continuity of Transactions Criterion" implies that a seller or a buyer, in his attempt to choose his transactions partner, exercises his judgement based on the amount of past and previous transactions; this tends to exclude those with whom he has done little or no business previously. This practice naturally leads to a long-term fixed mutual relationship between the seller and the buyer.

Suppose that a large retail merchandiser decides to add to his stores' merchandise an item never offered to him before, and no current transactions partner, be it a manufacturer or a wholesaler, carries that new item. He now has to look for a supplier of that item. Suppose he finds a manufacturer with whom he has never dealt before. Given that the "Order Quantity Criterion" is fully satisfied, this large retail firm often finds that, in Japan, it is unable to initiate a transaction with the newly found manufacturer-supplier. The supplier would attribute this reaction to the "Continuity of Transactions Criterion." Since the retail firm never conducted business with this supplier before, it does not meet, in the eyes of the manufacturer, the "Continuity of Transactions Criterion." Even if this retail firm is unable to buy the item directly from the manufacturer, this does not mean that it will never be able to deal in that item. If the growing retailer cannot add new items, the manufacturers of these items will lose out on the opportunity to expand their market. The manufacturer tries, in keeping with the "Continuity of Transactions Criterion," to bring this retailer into his sales network channels. He will introduce the retailer to the wholesaler (the business partner who satisfies the "Continuity Criterion") with whom he has been doing direct business, and will persuade the retailer to buy the item from the wholesaler.

Furthermore, the "Continuity of Transactions Criterion" is also applied by a buyer dealing with a supplier-seller. For example, suppose a new processed food manufacturer wishes to establish a sales relationship for a just-developed product with a large-scale retailer who judges carrying the product to be a useful merchandising strategy. The said manufacturer in this case does not meet the "Continuity of Transactions Criterion" of the retailer, therefore he cannot enter directly into a sales relationship with the retailer. This large-scale retailer, to develop a new purchasing channel for this product, introduces the wholesaler, with whom he has long been directly dealing, to the manufacturer, and guides the manufacturer in selling the product to him through this wholesaler. The large-scale retailer purchases the product in question from the wholesaler.

Some comments are in order here on the nature and application of the "Continuity of Transactions Criterion":

First, the application of the "Continuity Criterion" does not necessarily mean the automatic exclusion of a new business partner or a new entrant into the business relations. As was explained earlier in the examples, a manufacturer is making every effort to bring a large retail firm as his new business partner into his own well-established channel. A large retail firm also earnestly tries to bring a new entrant manufacturer, through a wholesaler he has an established business relationship with, into his own distribution channel.

Secondly, we must point out here that the "Continuity of Transactions Criterion" is not applied in today's Japan as an absolute criterion. Suppose that a manufacturer, who just got into the processed food industry with a highly differentiated, superior, and high value-added product, wanted to sell it directly to a large-scale retailer. In this type of situation, the retailer often decides not to adhere to the "Continuity of Transactions Criterion"; that is, he agrees to do transactions directly with the manufacturer, without going through the wholesaler. The retailer's decision is based on his judgement that the following kind of merits far outweigh the application of the criterion:

1. Due to high value added, the new product might turn out to be a major high profit item for the retailer if it does not go through a wholesaler taking in a sales margin.
2. The manufacturer is hoping to deal directly with us (the retailer). The degree of differentiation of the product is high, and therefore, seems to have competitive power. Considering our competition with other large-scale retailers, we would be advised to accept the offer. Competitive merits (or avoidance of demerits) are considerably large.

As noted above, the "Continuity of Transactions Criterion" often is judged, and applied flexibly, with other economic merits taken into account.

Rationale for "Continuity of Transactions Criterion"

Why does the "Continuity of Transactions Criterion" exist, and what should be the rationale for its existence?

First, in Japan, before a transaction can take place, an established relationship of mutual trust is required. An established relationship of mutual trust implies that:

1. The frequency and extent of conflicting interests are kept at a minimum.
2. If and when a conflict develops between the two parties, the possibility of resolving that conflict internally is maximized.

For two parties to arrive at such a state, a great amount of communication is needed for both parties to truly understand each other. It can be said that the "Continuity of Transactions Criterion" springs from the need for extensive communications between the two parties.

Secondly, if there is an established relationship of 'mutual trust,' then the cost of individual transactions will be reduced.[5] For example, it is not necessary to prepare a complicated contract in anticipation of serious conflict between the two mutually trusting parties. Also, the amount of time necessary for reaching a contract agreement is shortened. Moreover, court-related expenses incurred related to failed transactions, insurance premiums, and the like will be minimized.

Thirdly, the "Continuity of Transactions Criterion" helps to contain the number of transaction partners for the firm. This leads to smaller numbers of individual transactions, thus helping to control the growing total cost of transactions.[6]

SOME CHARACTERISTICS OF TRANSACTION TERMS PECULIAR TO JAPAN

Categorizing Transaction Terms

The terms and conditions of product distribution transactions may be categorized as follows:

1. Those relevant to the product and its transfer (delivery).
   Quality standards, delivery dates and the return policy for unsold goods will be included in this section.
2. Sales rewards, promotions ~ so-called rebates.
   Rebate occurs when the seller returns a percentage of a product's sales proceeds to the buyer because the buyer has placed large enough orders to expand the market, or the buyer has otherwise assisted the seller.
3. Supplementary services related to selling.
   In order to increase sales the seller often offers supplementary services to the buyer. Some of these services are specifically included in the terms of transactions.

Transactional Terms and Conditions for Products and Their Transfer

The basic terms of the transactions concern mainly the quality of the product and delivery. In Japan the buyer imposes on the seller very stringent conditions concerning quality standards and delivery time. These two issues create the most disputes in negotiations between the buyer and the seller. The seller often tries to resolve the problem by accepting the buyer's stringent requirements to a great extent, as long as the product is not in the "seller's market." There may be two reasons for this flexibility on the seller's part. First, as already stated, establishment and development of a relationship of mutual trust through the continuation of transactions is considered in Japan to be of utmost importance. The buyer bases his decision on whether or not to continue a business relationship with the seller dependent upon the quality of the product and timing of delivery. These two factors concurrently determine the degree of success with which the seller can establish and maintain a relationship of mutual trust with the buyer. Secondly, there is a strong tendency for the seller in Japan not only to think of the immediate buyer as his customer, but also to look beyond the buyer to the ultimate consumer. For example, a manufacturer who sells his product directly to a large retail chain tries, in collaboration and in joint effort with the retailer, to obtain household consumers as their customers. The retail chain bases its rigorous quality and delivery requirements according to household consumer demand. Knowing this full well, the manufacturer is already psychologically prepared to accept the stringent retailer requirements.

The strictness of quality and delivery conditions reflects the stringency of the quality control level and inventory control in Japanese firms. On the other hand, maintaining such strict conditions is psychological "proof" of the development and maintenance of the "relationship of mutual trust and confidence" between seller and buyer.

Next, we will make a few observations on returned goods by the buyer. In the U.S. and Europe, a sale of a product implies the transfer of title or possession of the product from the seller to the buyer, so return of goods cannot be accepted, unless these goods are defective or deficient in some way. In Japan, however, return of goods sold, tacitly or through mutual negotiations, may be accepted. For example, if the merchandise is displayed on the retailer's shelf for as long as three months, the retailer will try to return the goods to the seller. In this case, the seller has no choice but to accept them. There are two reasons for this practice. First, there is a belief in Japan that, even after the transfer of possession of the product from a manufacturer to a retailer, if the product remains unsold on the retailer's shelf, it may not be best to let the retailer alone bear the burden of not being able to sell it. Neither the manufacturer nor the retailer has prior perfect knowledge as to what extent particular merchandise will sell. A certain amount of uncertainty always remains. In the U.S. and Europe, as soon as the merchandise is transferred to the buyer, the seller no longer has to worry about the uncertainty of whether or not the goods will be sold. However, the Japanese do not fully accept this view. This element of uncertainty is to be resolved within the context of the "relationship of mutual trust."

Secondly, most Japanese manufacturers do not resort to test marketing a new product. Instead, they introduce a new product directly into the market. They then, evaluate the product's market potential on the basis of actual selling performance, and decide whether to improve or discard it. This type of practice is evidence of the severity of competition when introducing a new product into the Japanese market. With this practice, the manufacturer evaluates the product's market potential in view of the returns of unsold goods from the buyer. In other words, return of goods is taking the place of test marketing.[7]

Reward-Sales Promotional Terms of Transactions—
So-Called "Rebates"

In Japan, as part of business transactions, the seller gives the buyer a number of rebates. We classify these rebates as follows:

1. Quantity Rebates

    These are rebates paid according to the quantity of the buyer's order. There are two kinds, depending upon how the quantity is measured:

    a. Order size rebates: rebates paid according to the size of each order.

    b. Rebates for total quantity ordered through the period: rebates paid for the total cumulative amount of orders in a predetermined period.

    Usually either (a) or (b) is employed, but there are cases where both are used.

2. Payment Date Rebates

    These are rebates paid to the buyer who makes payment on or before the due date.

3. Target Achievement Rebates

    This rebate is paid according to what degree the buyer has met the seller's agreed upon targets for the coming period, in areas like total sales and new customers. These include sales rebates (paid according to the percentage met of the sales target for a particular product line), new product rebates (paid according to the percentage met of the sales target for a newly introduced product), new cus-

tomer rebates (paid according to what degree the buyer met the target for generating a number of new customers).
  4. Physical Distribution Rebates
       The seller pays these rebates to the buyer who assists the seller with the physical distribution of the goods ordered, or who agrees to do it on behalf of the seller. For example, there are rebates for small individual packaging and delivery (the seller pays the buyer who, at the request of the seller, makes small packages and delivers them to the buyer's individual customers); repackaging rebates (paid to the buyer, who at the request of the seller, makes a special small package and/or inspects and repacks); inventory burden rebates (paid to the buyer who, at the request of the seller, shares the burden and cost of special inventory).
  5. Sales Promotion Rebates
       These are various rebates paid to the buyer who shares the work/cost or in some way cooperates with the seller who wishes to put on sales promotional programs (POP, displays, sales campaigns, etc.).
  6. Special Rebates
       These are the rebates paid to the buyer based on the seller's overall evaluation of how much the buyer contributed to the seller's business.

A few points of observations regarding the rebate system are as follows:
First, the U.S. and Europe possess only two comparable practices, that is, the order size rebates [(a) listed], and the on-time payment date rebates [(2) listed]. In comparison, one can easily see the variety and multitude of rebates in the Japanese system.
Secondly, rebates in the U.S. and Europe take the form of immediate discounts. That is, the seller subtracts from the bill the amount of rebates to determine how much the buyer owes, or the buyer takes the rebate (discount) and pays the billed amount minus the rebate. In most cases in Japan, by contrast, the total amount of rebates are paid at the end of each accounting period (normally one full year, or every half year), or at the end of a certain pre-fixed, agreed upon period of three or six months. Actually, it would be difficult for the seller to pay each piece of rebates, in view of the variety and nature of these rebates, in the form of immediate discounts, except for the order size rebates and on-time payment date rebates. For rebate items (b), (3) and (6), both parties have to wait until the end of the period before they know how much to pay and receive. Items (4) and (5) are not directly linked to a sale of a particular unit of merchandise. These two items are to be evaluated period by period, based on which rebates are more efficiently calculated.

Transactional Conditions for Supplementary Service

With a view to expand the market for his products in Japan, the seller is usually in a position to have to provide various kinds of services to the buyer. Some of these services make up part of the transactional agreement. "Supplementary Services" are those services contained in the agreement. Generally speaking, there is no payment directly linked to a specific item of services provided. One must notice that since there is no direct payment for some of these services, this means that there will be a need for adjustment in the other terms and conditions in the transaction agreement. For example, the buyer makes bill payment earlier than scheduled, or the seller makes less than due rebates to the buyer. There are situations where this kind of adjustment may not be enough to compensate the seller for the amount of services offered.

Here are a few examples of these Supplementary Services:

1. Dispatched Sales Help:
   Manufacturers or wholesalers dispatch to the department store some of their employees to help with sales efforts on store sales floors. These employees handle only the products of their employer company. The department store receives free labor when it comes to selling the products of the dispatcher company. The dispatched sales personnel handle such merchandise as apparel, arts and craft objects, expensive dinnerware, and high-class candies.
2. Price Tagging Operations:
   On behalf of large store chains, wholesalers put price tags on each unit of merchandise before delivery, usually at the wholesaler's site. How much to charge at the store gets relayed to wholesalers just prior to shipment.
3. Substantial Physical Distribution and Repackaging:
   In Japan, the wholesaler has great responsibility. For example, when the retailer owns two or more stores, the wholesaler is often responsible for breaking the bulk order, repackaging the shipment according to the specific needs of the retailer's stores, and for delivering it to each store.

These Supplementary Services may be classified into two categories:

First, those which can be seen in a "buyers market." The seller is forced into agreeing to the buyer's demands for services. When competition gets keen in Japan, the seller has a tendency to seek recognition from the buyer by increasing and attaching additional supplementary services, gratis. This is why such practices prevail.

The second reason involves the kind of services the seller is willing to provide, even without demands or requests from the buyer, as an active sales strategy. As pointed out, the seller in Japan has an inclination to work together with the buyer to approach the consumers. This helps to explain the active use of these promotional services. Apparel manufacturers, for example, develop their skills and learn how to grasp current trends and most recent changes in customer preferences through the sales help dispatch system to the department store. This practice is believed to have contributed significantly to the substantial growth of those manufacturers. These apparel manufacturers employ "Sales Personnel Dispatch Systems" as one of their important marketing strategies.

Rationale for Diversity and Variety of Transaction Terms

As has been pointed out earlier, Japan's transactional terms are diverse. The establishment and maintenance of the "relationship of mutual trust" acts as a supporting backdrop to these various practices. Here we would like to explain the relationship between these two aspects of Japanese business, the diversity of transaction terms and the "relationship of mutual trust."

First, the fact is that the establishment and maintenance of mutual trust relationship requires the diversity of these transactional terms and conditions. For both partners to establish and maintain the relationship of mutual trust, it is necessary for them to minimize mutual confrontations and to maximize cooperation. To do that, each of them must be in a position to feel "if I lose in this aspect, I know I will gain in another aspect." This kind of situation may only be created by having a great variety of transactional terms and conditions. For example, a manufacturer may feel he can reduce the amount of rebates to a retailer, who demands extremely stringent quality and delivery conditions. In this way, the manufacturer avoids serious confrontation and continues to cooperate with the retailer. If only quality and delivery conditions and no rebate clause exist, in their mutual agreement, the manufacturer will have a hard time finding a way out. In this sense, establishment and maintenance of a mutual trust relationship need the variety and diversity of transactional terms.

Second is the fact that conversely, the variety and diversity of transactional terms need the establishment and maintenance of the relationship of mutual trust. Each item in the agreement, in most cases, is with the contingency that if condition A exists, then B may be claimed. Each individual transactional condition, in most cases, is within the contract and takes the conditional form "if condition A holds, then B may be claimed." The fact that transactional conditions are diverse means that both parties must reach an agreement to a contract containing mutually intertwined, and rather complicated clauses. For two parties simply to maintain a buying and selling business relationship, they must sign a rather detailed and complicated contract. The making of these documents requires painstaking effort. For both parties to agree on even one item within the contract consumes a significant amount of time. The diversity and variety of transactional terms require the establishment and maintenance of the relationship of mutual trust that will enable both parties to handle and dispose of contract matters efficiently and at a low cost.[8]

FORMALITY OF TRANSACTION AGREEMENT

We will analyze the degree of formality within the transaction agreement in Japan by analyzing to what extent the contents of the agreement are actually documented. We will elaborate on the conclusion that in Japan the documentation of the agreement between business partners is limited in general, and is concentrated within a few areas. For example, if one is allowed to see a contract agreement and the attached supplements made by a processed food manufacturer and its wholesaler, he will be able to see the following characteristics:

1. The contract, generally and in principle, presumes that the mutual transactions and business relationship will continue at least one year as an annual contract. Some of the contracts explicitly state in the preamble that these two parties will engage in regular or nearly regular scheduled sales transactions. In other words, the contract itself has a tendency towards fostering long-term business relationships.
2. The contract document usually runs as long as two regular-size pages, double or sometimes triple spaced. It consists of ten or so items, written in simple general sentences. A few of those items, however, have supplementary attachments where technical details are specified. In the Japanese contract those areas of importance have supplements attached to them.
3. Those main items usually covered in the contract are such things as "Products Covered," "Target Sales (item by item)," "Payment Due Dates," "Rebates," and "Supplementary Services." Detailed supplements are usually attached to "Rebates." The contract states "which party does what." Except for the "Payment Due Dates," there is no mention of "In the event that such and such happens . . ." in anticipation of some future uncertain events. However, the last item in the contract usually is a catch-all term for all these uncertain eventualities that says that "if something unspecified in the contract

and unanticipated by either party occurs, it will be resolved in full spirit of cooperation and with mutual trust and confidence through the joint effort by both parties." Very rarely do "Quality" and "Delivery time" get mentioned in the contract. In regards to "Quality," if it has to be taken up, it is taken up by a separate technical supplementary piece of document.

4. As to "Rebates," they are also dealt with in a separate supplementary document, since they include a wide range of types and a complicated set of numbers.

From the previous discussion, it is clear that the documentation of agreement in Japan puts emphasis on those events low in uncertainty and high in complexity, as is indicated in Figure 1.

From the fact that the documentation is concentrated in rather small areas it may be safely said that the degree of formality of transactions in Japan is fairly low. In other words, in only those cases which fall in the fourth quadrant in Figure 1, the direction of behavior is clear in a preset, formal manner. Each of the cases which fall in other quadrants will be dealt with separately and independently at each occurrence through mutual negotiation and a cooperative effort, or else there has already been an agreed upon, tacit understanding in an unspecified way about how to get such cases settled. If a smooth functioning relationship continues in such an undefined and unstructured environment, then what makes it all possible must again be the existence of the well-established and well-maintained "relationship of mutual trust."

One additional point may be mentioned here that indicates a low degree of formality of transactions in Japan. That is the fact that business relations are based on managers' personal relationships. One of these typical cases

FIGURE 1

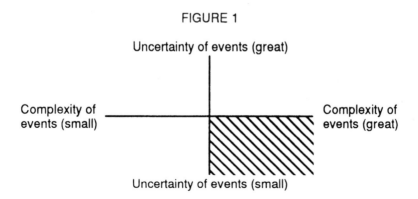

Uncertainty of events (great)

Complexity of events (small)　　　　　　　　　　　Complexity of events (great)

Uncertainty of events (small)

is the situation in which two individuals representing respective negotiating firms come first to agreement in principle through their rather close
personal relationship, then work toward company-wide, mutual agreement. When a firm in negotiations is not sure if it can successfully con-
summate a business deal with a partner, it tries to eliminate disputes and
stumbling blocks one by one, and tries to make transaction terms more and
more diverse as necessary toward furthering mutual cooperation. This is
done through personal contact between participating managers. Two
points of importance are in order here.[9] The first is that the establishment
and maintenance of the "relationship of mutual trust" makes it essential
for the participating managers to have personal contact with each other.
Also critically important is frequent communications between them. This
means that manager(s) at both firms must frequently keep in touch with
each other. There is a limit to how much both partner firms can increase
mutual contact and interaction. "Interfirm Relationship" must depend for
the most part upon the very close personal relationship between people at
each firm. The second point is that the original individual, although he
may have been promoted or rotated, comes to the support of his successor
whenever his assistance is needed in smoothly running relations between
firms. In Japan, there is an apparatus that makes this continued relationship possible. The lifetime employment system in Japanese firms allows
the same individual to stay with his firm for a long time. Even after an
intrafirm job rotation, managers in Japan try to keep contact with the
manager partner on a personal level, and to maintain a personal relationship. In this way, their firms can maintain future business relations with
each other. Both parties form expectations that the relationship will get
stronger through promotion of the managers involved. These expectations
are realizable under Japan's seniority system. The continued personal
relationship after the relocation of a manager with his partner enables
smooth communications between the new managers during transitions and
afterwards. This is because a relocated manager is usually, due to the
seniority system, senior to a manager newly assigned to the post, and is in
a position to convey his message and transmit to the new manager his
intentions, purposes, and what he and their firm want to accomplish in the
relationship with the other firm.

CONTINUITY AND DURABILITY
OF TRANSACTIONAL RELATIONS

Our analysis up to this point has indicated that transactional relations in
Japan are assumed to last for long periods of time. First of all, the develop-

ment and maintenance of the "relationship of mutual trust" assumes a long-lasting business relationship. Secondly, such things as the application of "Continuity of Transactions Criterion," end-of-the-period payment of rebates, and annual contracts reiterate and reinforce long-term relationships.

The long-term transactional relationship is not condition-fixational in the sense of constraining and getting fixed on how transactions are conducted in the long-term. It is rather condition-adaptive, in the sense that both parties assume that their business relationship will continue in the future, and they are ready and prepared to adapt themselves to newly changing environments by varying their transactions patterns and behavior.[10] This is why contract documents sealed towards long-term business relationships, are devoid of these items involving anticipated future uncertainties. This is in sharp contrast with contracts found in the U.S. and Europe, which attempt to account for any and every imaginable eventuality in the uncertain world of mutual business transactions, in the search for stability in the relationship between both parties.

THE PATTERN OF TRANSACTION COST AND THE BARRIER TO ENTRY

Finally, we compare the pattern of transaction cost in Japan with that in the U.S. and Europe, and refer to how Japanese business practices may be the entry-barrier from foreigners' viewpoints.

As often mentioned already, Japanese business practices are based upon the "relationship of mutual trust," which requires many cumulative transactions. The more the amount of these transactions, the lower each transaction cost. But it requires a lot of effort and time for a newcomer to reach the stage where he can use the experience in transactions effectively towards the "relationship of mutual trust." That is, in the early stages, one transaction's cost in Japan is relatively high, and later on it becomes lower and lower. Perhaps, this pattern doesn't apply in the U.S. and Europe. In Figure 2, we can consider line A as the transaction cost curve in Japan, and line B as the one in the U.S. and Europe.

Now, the area bounded by the left-side of the line A and the upper-side of the line B can be considered as the entry-barrier from the newcomer's viewpoint.[11] This entry-barrier may be eliminated through the newcomer's introduction into market of excellent products and services, and the cost for getting over this barrier can be compensated later by reaching the degree at which he cuts transaction costs through establishing the "relationship of mutual trust."

FIGURE 2

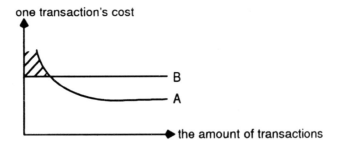

NOTES

1. For example, we can acknowledge Sangyo Institute (1980), Sumitomo Business Consulting (1983), Tajima and Miyashita (1985), Kondo and Nakano (1985), and Tamura (1986).

2. Among the studies mentioned above, Sumitomo Business Consulting (1980) and Tamura (1986) refer to Japanese transaction usage. But the former describes only abstract facts and lacks systematic analysis. The latter tries to establish a comprehensive model, but lacks collection and analysis of the facts.

3. These field studies were conducted at the following times:
   January 20, 1987–January 30, 1987
   March 2, 1987–March 7, 1987
   May 18, 1987–May 23, 1987

4. About these four dimensions, see Arakawa (1983).

5. This idea is based on the "theory of transaction cost," cf. Williamson (1975).

6. This idea, if explored, can lead to the "minimization of total transaction numbers," cf. Hall (1971).

7. The same point was made in Conference on Comparative Studies of Vertical Marketing System (1986).

8. See Tamura (1986).

9. The same point was made in Tamura (1986).

10. See Tamura (1986).

11. The same point was made in Tamura (1986).

REFERENCES

Arakawa, Yukichi (1983), *Principles of Commerce* (Japanese), Chuokeizaisha.

Conference on Comparative Studies of Vertical Marketing System (1986), *Comparative Study of Distribution Structure and Transaction Patterns, and Competitive* (Japanese), Fair Trade Commission in Japan.

Hall, M. (1971), "The Theory of Wholesale Distribution" in W.G. Moller, Jr. and D.L. Wilemon (eds). *Marketing Channels : A System Viewpoint*. Irwin.

Kondo, Fumio and Yasushi Nakano (1985), *Distribution Structure and Marketing Channel* (Japanese). Minelva Shobo.

Sangyo Institute (1980), *International Comparative Study of Distribution Structure* (Japanese), Sangyo Institute.

Sumitomo Business Consulting (1983), *International Comparative Study of Distribution Structure and Transaction Usage* (Japanese), Sumitomo Business Consulting Co.

Tajima, Yoshihiro and Masafusa Miyashita (1985), *International Comparative Study of Distribution* (Japanese), Yuhikaku.

Tamura, Masanori (1986). *Japanese Distribution System* (Japanese). Chikura Shobo.

Toys "R" Us Fuels Changes in Japan's Toy-Distribution System

Yoshio Takahashi

SUMMARY. Toys "R" Us is one of the first foreign retail chains to target the mass market in Japan. It introduces its successful formula that includes self-service, everyday low prices, high volume, a large scale and a vast selection of merchandise. Referred to as a category killer store format, this is an approach new to Japan. It has also brought a method of dealing directly with manufacturers as a means of cutting costs in support of its discount strategy. These characteristics are revolutionary to Japan, especially to the toy-distribution system's traditional characteristics. For foreign manufacturers, Toys "R" Us has also provided a new channel to sidestep Japan's complicated distribution system. As such, its arrival has introduced fierce competition destined to accelerate changes in the Japanese toy-distribution system.

INTRODUCTION

In December 1991, Toys "R" Us launched its first giant and the first-ever American toy retail chain-store in Japan. On opening day, it was crowded by some 17,000 shoppers, while the chain's second store was inaugurated

---

Yoshio Takahashi is Senior Researcher at the Distribution Economics Institute of Japan.

Address correspondence to: The Distribution Economics Institute of Japan, c/o Yoshio Takahashi, the 3rd TOC Building, 7-23-1 Nishi-Gotanda, Tokyo, 141 Japan.

[Haworth co-indexing entry note]: "Toys "R" Us Fuels Changes in Japan's Toy-Distribution System." Takahashi, Yoshio. Co-published simultaneously in the *Journal of Marketing Channels* (The Haworth Press, Inc.) Vol. 3, No. 3, 1994, pp. 91-112; and: *Japanese Distribution Channels* (ed: Takeshi Kikuchi) The Haworth Press, Inc., 1994, pp. 91-112. Multiple copies of this article/chapter may be purchased from The Haworth Document Delivery Center [1-800-3-HAWORTH; 9:00 a.m. - 5:00 p.m. (EST)].

by former U.S. President George Bush amid much fanfare. Less than happy, Japan's small toy retailers called Toys "R" Us the "Black Ship" of American large-scale retailing–in reference to the 19th-century traders who forced Japan to open its markets.

The first Toys "R" Us opened after three years of negotiation. The chain's penetration was timely in that it had the support of the modified Large-Scale Retail Store Law, effected following SII (Structural Impediment Initiative between the U.S. and Japan) talks. The modification of the Law looked as the symbol of a new openness of the Japanese market and its distribution system to foreign companies.

Termed a category killer, Toys "R" Us didn't enter as a niche brand goods retailer but rather as one of the first foreign retail chains in Japan to target the mass market. Unlike typical Japanese chain stores, it has its own distribution center and trucks, providing the capability to supply its stores itself. In bypassing Japan's wholesalers and suppliers in this way to directly deal with toy manufacturers, the chain is able to cut costs to gain a big competitive advantage in their everyday low price discount strategy, something unheard of in the Japanese toy market. Japan's toy-distribution system has some typical characteristics of Japan's distribution system, such as a fragmented retail structure, multiple layers of wholesale functions, and business practices specific to merchandise (e.g., Czinkota 1985, Goldman 1991). It could thus serve as a good example to describe this traditional Japanese distribution system.

The purpose of this paper is to provide a case study for the proper understanding of how the distribution system works and how it is changing in Japan. In doing so, we will look at the recent Toys "R" Us entry in the Japanese market, how it has gained penetration, and what the effect has been on the toy-distribution system in Japan.

For discussion's sake, the paper has been organized into four sections. The first outlines the characteristics of the toy market, distribution structure, and business practices in Japan prior to Toys "R" Us. The second section concentrates on the Toys "R" Us strategy for penetrating the Japanese market. The third focuses on the various responses to its entry from different concerns in the distribution system. The fourth provides a summary and looks into trends in the changing toy-distribution system in Japan.

JAPAN'S TOY-DISTRIBUTION SYSTEM

This section looks at the toy-distribution system and its changing dynamics in Japan prior to Toys "R" Us. The Section consists of four parts: the characteristics of the toy market, distribution channels, the retail structure, and business practices.

Characteristics

The toy market in Japan generates sales of more than ¥800 billion annually (1991), the world's second largest market after the United States. Of this, the TV game market's estimated worth is about ¥300 billion. In the 60s and 70s, the Japanese toy industry was primarily export-oriented, with 80% of products exported and the remaining 20% distributed within the domestic market. The domestic toy market was thus still relatively small. Even so, a basic distribution system was in place, and in the toy market, manufacturers enjoyed a relatively strong position. Then, with the unfolding of the oil crisis in the 70s, the yen's appreciation in the 80s, and with world competition, the industry was gradually transformed.

The characteristics of Japan's toy market have nevertheless generally remained unchanged and reflect the characteristics of the toys themselves. A similarity can also be observed in the distribution system. That is, the toy market has generally been one of high risk, low prices, low inventory turnover, and higher rates for seasonal and faddish or fashionable merchandise compared with commodity merchandise such as food or general merchandise. During the Christmas and New Year holiday season, toy sales account for about 40% of annual sales.

The market is divided into three submarkets: traditional (basic) toys, character goods, and TV games. Other than basic toys and TV games, many toys are designed using popular TV cartoon characters to attract children. These so-called "character goods" have relatively short life cycles according to a character's popularity.

Products in the fast-growing TV game market demonstrate the same tendency towards relatively short life cycles depending on their attractiveness. But it can be considered a different market. As a software-oriented one, the product market value is changeable and depends on consumer preference. It's a higher risk market. This creates a fast-growing and different production and distribution system specific to TV games.

As stated above, the toy market is generally characterized as high risk, largely dependent on seasonality, product popularity, fads, and fashions. Market growth is thus heavily reliant on manufacturer creativity in providing new products and TV advertising. Moreover, the fragmented retail structure, as will be discussed later, has also remained limited to minimize risk in carrying inventory. Manufacturers, to reduce risk, tend to determine production quantity based on past results. This tendency makes it difficult for manufacturers to respond quickly to a repeat order when a product achieves popularity more than pre-estimated. It's a difficult market to predict. Simply stated, the toy market and distribution system can generally be characterized as involving high-risk seasonal and popular merchandise requiring a wide variety and small quantities. It also strongly favors manufacturers' initiative.

Distribution Channels

The toy-distribution channels are shown in Figure 1. There are about 100 manufacturers, including 10 large brand-name makers such as Bandai, Takara, Epoch, etc. Most products are supplied by manufacturers to wholesalers and then resold to retailers.

The wholesale stage is divided into two layers, with the first consisting of 400 primary wholesalers. These entities generally provide a full line of

FIGURE 1

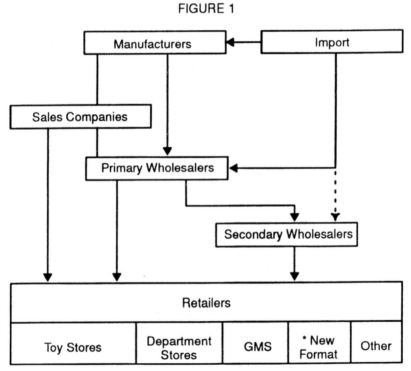

* Toy-specialty chain
Source: Modified *Monthly Toy Journal*

toy merchandise, which they supply to some 1,000 local companies (estimated about 4,000 establishments).

At the retail stage, there are 29,413 establishments that sell toys, including department stores, general merchandise stores (GMS), and toy stores. Toy stores account for 15,243 establishments and generate ¥714 billion in annual sales–nearly 87% of the total retail sales in Japan (1991).

Most foreign toys are imported by primary wholesalers, manufacturers, and other importers. Of these, major wholesalers such as Tsukuda and Kawada play the larger roles in distribution, enjoying licensing contracts or sole-agency contracts with foreign manufacturers. They also supply imported toys to retailers through the same distribution channels as for domestic toys. In addition, some foreign manufacturers have chosen to establish subsidiaries in Japan. Mattel, for example, has just launched its fourth trial attempt to establish a sales subsidiary.

The distribution of TV game products, however, through the existing toy-distribution system is rapidly decreasing and now estimated less than 50% of the market. This segment has increasingly become part of the computer and new-media market, and the TV-game software-distribution channel now includes discount stores, personal computer shops, and specialty stores.

Retail Structure

The retail structure mainly consists of some 15,000 toy stores (1991), and as such is quite fragmented compared to only 9,629 (1987) in the United States. Most of these toy stores (99%) have less than 500 sq. m. of selling space, avoiding the required complicated process under the Large-Scale Retail Store Law to open a store. Moreover, 88% of all stores are less than 200 sq. m. in size, yet account for some 60% of all sales (Table 1). In terms of personnel, those stores with less than five employees account for 87% of all establishments and generate some 53% of total sales (Table 2).

These figures show that in Japan small shops have managed to survive despite the growth of chain stores (Goldman 1991 and Kakeda 1992). Recent surveys, however, have shown some structural changes in retailing. The traditional unincorporated smaller toy stores, especially the smallest in size of employees, are sharply decreasing (Table 3). Over a nine-year period, unincorporated–mom-and-pop stores–decreased by 16% (Table 4). While total number of stores decreased, most of the increases seen were among incorporated stores. Similarly, size increases in terms of employee numbers were also limited to incorporated stores except larger unincorporated stores with five to nine employees. Clearly, the retail struc-

TABLE 1

Selling space	Establishments				Sales			
	1982	1991	1982 (%)	1991 (%)	1982 (mil. yen)	1991 (mil. yen)	1982 (%)	1991 (%)
Total	16,605	15,243	100	100	383,036	714,657	100	100
– 10 m² (under)	809	403	4.87	2.64	3,067	3,114	0.80	0.44
10 m² – 20 m²	3,600	1,955	21.68	12.83	21,646	21,571	5.65	3.02
20 m² – 30 m²	3,304	2,188	19.90	14.35	30,511	34,169	7.97	4.78
30 m² – 50 m²	3,904	3,732	23.51	24.48	59,747	96,014	15.60	13.43
50 m² – 100 m²	3,002	3,502	18.08	22.97	91,525	149,793	23.89	20.96
100 m² – 200 m²	1,344	1,694	8.09	11.11	81,177	144,900	21.19	20.28
200 m² – 500 m²	531	1,379	3.20	9.05	59,844	189,084	15.62	26.46
500 m² – 1000 m²	59	76	0.36	0.50	16,092	17,666	4.20	2.47
1000 m² – 1500 m²	11	22	0.07	0.14	x	11,487	x	1.61
1500 m² – 3000 m²	1	8	0.01	0.05	x	12,630	x	1.77
3000 m² –	1	2	0.01	0.01	x	x	x	x
Not reported	39	282	x	x	9,991	x	2.61	x

Source: Census of Commerce

TABLE 2

No. of Employees	Establishments				Annual Sales			
	1982	1991	1982 (%)	1991 (%)	1982 (mil. yen)	1991 (mil. yen)	1982 (%)	1991 (%)
Total	16,605	15,243	100.0	100.0	383,036	714,657	100.0	100.0
1 – 2	12,420	9,501	74.8	62.3	113,995	168,233	29.8	23.5
3 – 4	2,912	3,735	17.5	24.5	108,872	208,725	28.4	29.2
5 – 9	1,052	1,660	6.3	10.9	96,450	202,530	25.2	28.3
10 – 19	186	273	1.1	1.8	40,108	79,885	10.5	11.2
20 – 29	26	47	0.2	0.3	15,253	20,532	4.0	2.9
30 – 49	7	21	0.0	0.1	x	17,353	x	2.4
50 – 99	2	4	0.0	0.0	x	x	x	x
100 –	0	2	0.0	0.0	–	x	–	x

Source: Census of Commerce

TABLE 3

Establishments / No. of Employees	1982			1991		
	Total	Incorporated	Unincorporated	Total	Incorporated	Unincorporated
Total	16,605	3,431	13,174	15,243	5,781	9,642
1 – 2	12,420	1,137	11,283	9,501	1,805	7,696
3 – 4	2,912	1,296	1,616	3,735	2,248	1,487
5 – 9	1,052	801	251	1,660	1,398	262
10 – 19	186	166	20	273	261	12
20 – 29	26	23	3	47	43	4
30 – 49	7	6	1	21	20	1
50 – 99	2	2	0	4	4	x
100 –	0	0	0	2	2	x

Source: Census of Commerce

TABLE 4

Establishments No. of Employees	1982			1991		
	Total	Incorporated	Unincorporated	Total	Incorporated	Unincorporated
Total	100.0 (%)	20.7 (%)	79.3 (%)	100.0 (%)	37.9 (%)	63.3 (%)
1 – 2	74.8	6.8	67.9	62.3	11.8	50.5
3 – 4	17.5	7.8	9.7	24.5	14.7	9.8
5 – 9	6.3	4.8	1.5	10.9	9.2	1.7
10 – 19	1.1	1.0	0.1	1.8	1.7	0.1
20 – 29	0.2	0.1	0.0	0.3	0.3	0.0
30 – 49	0.0	0.0	0.0	0.1	0.1	0.0
50 – 99	0.0	0.0	0.0	0.0	0.0	0.0
100 –	0.0	0.0	0.0	0.0	0.0	0.0

Source: Census of Commerce

ture is rapidly shifting towards incorporated stores, and shop size is increasing in numbers of employees.

The growing sectors in toy retailing type of stores are GMSs and toy-specialty chain stores (Table 5). There are currently two large toy-specialty chains, Hello Mac and Ban Ban. Considered as new store formats, both chains were established by shoe-retail chains in the mid-80s. Targeting the untouched suburban market, their relatively large stores (330 sq. m. overage) can be found along major roads in the suburbs. Most customers are auto-oriented suburban shoppers.

GMSs are Japan's leading chain stores, such as Ito-Yokado, Daiei, Jasco, etc. They offer a wide variety of merchandise for one-stop shopping. Utilizing POS-based, sophisticated information systems, emphasis is placed on efficiency of merchandising and product lines, generally targeting only fast-moving items. Conversely, most small traditional toy stores' merchandising is limited and heavily dependent upon wholesalers.

Similarly, department-store merchandising is also heavily dependent on wholesalers for domestic goods. Their selections are also limited and prices are relatively high because of the services clerks provide and because of the gift market. These factors have led to the recent decline in department-store business. Nevertheless, although competition among retailers forces weaker ones out of the market, pricing was not the major factor until recently. The reason lies in the business practices related to the distribution structure.

Business Practices

As stated earlier, the leading characteristic of Japan's toy market has been the strong initiative of manufacturers. Manufacturers, wholesalers, and retailers form loose organization-like relationships based on long-term trade partnerships (Shimaguchi and Lazer 1979, Kakeda 1992, and Manifold 1993). Each role in distribution resembles a vertical division of functions. Manufacturers concentrate to develop new products and advertise accordingly. Distribution is heavily dependent upon primary and secondary wholesalers who supply merchandise throughout the spectrum from chain stores to small retail shops. Wholesalers even provide financial support to enable small shops to carry their merchandise. In a way, the vertical-distribution system is a risk-sharing system.

Many chain stores in Japan, unlike those in other industrialized countries, purchase their merchandise through wholesalers. Toy distribution is no exception. Not only toy-specialty chains but also GMSs purchase through wholesalers because they have no physical-distribution capability. Utilizing the wholesalers' physical-distribution function, instead of elimi-

TABLE 5

Type of stores	Sales share (%)	Trend	Store example
Toy stores	48.9	↗	Traditional small stores
GMSs	17.6	↖	Ito-Yokado, Daiei, Jusco, etc.
Department stores	14.3	↗	Matsuya, Mitsukoshi, etc.
New store formats	14.2	↖	Hello Mac, Ban Ban, etc.
Miniature model stores	5.0	↗	Traditional small stores
Total	100.0		

Source: Shogyokai (Jan. 1989)

nating intermediaries, chain stores have provided opportunities for whole-salers to proliferate. This also has helped small shops that are connected to wholesalers.

The typical pricing structure by the layer of each distribution stage is shown in Figure 2.

This pricing structure is based on the above distribution channels that sell through wholesalers. It doesn't change with quantity inasmuch as the wholesale price includes delivery to each shop. There thus exists no signif-icant quantity benefit for wholesalers because they have to deliver to each store no matter what distance. If this theory applies, retail pricing has limited scope to differentiate among retailers.

Until recently most of the toys sold at retail shops were priced at manufacturers' suggested prices. Japan hardly saw discounted prices be-fore Toys "R" Us. In this pricing structure, the manufacturers' strong initiative can be seen. As stated earlier, the toy market has high risks. The manufacturers therefore must maintain a high margin for the distributor and try to maintain a pricing strategy. This pricing structure tends to avoid price competition. It seems that the pricing structure is enhanced by the financial ties among the manufacturers, wholesalers, and retailers.

Toy manufacturers' and wholesalers' payment conditions are set to provide financial support to their customers and to enhance their relation-ships. Wholesalers' payments to manufacturers are generally made at half the invoice in cash and the remainder in 30- to 60-day promissory notes. Retailers' payments to wholesalers vary by trade. Small toy shops gener-ally pay partially in cash and the rest later in cash, usually after sale of the merchandise. The specialty chains, Hello Mac and Ban Ban, pay by 100-day promissory notes. GMSs and department stores pay by cash.

FIGURE 2

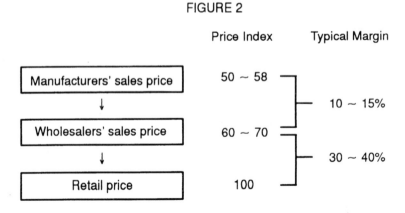

	Price Index	Typical Margin
Manufacturers' sales price	50 ~ 58	
↓		10 ~ 15%
Wholesalers' sales price	60 ~ 70	
↓		30 ~ 40%
Retail price	100	

Other than payment conditions, in some cases, large wholesalers take the risk and accept unsold returns from retailers. Rebates paid by the manufacturers to the wholesalers are much smaller compared to food or general merchandise.

These business practices have enabled manufacturers to distribute their merchandise to small stores and have enhanced the strong, vertical-distribution organic function. For the smaller retailers, this has enabled survival despite competition (Goldman 1991 and Kakeda 1992). This system has worked well to maintain a stable, continuing relationship.

It is true, however, that this system–a somewhat exclusive relationship among retailers, wholesalers, and manufacturers–tends to present a barrier to newcomers. This was proved, for example, even regarding the Japanese retailer Hello Mac, a specialty chain established in the mid-80s. Its startup was not easy. The first obstacle was to obtain enough merchandise to fill its shelves. This was because wholesalers' supplies were based on past records and continuous relations. Hello Mac therefore started with few fast-moving popular products. Today, Hello Mac has more than 350 stores and annual sales exceeding ¥53 billion. It has become fully capable of early buying from manufacturers at toy exhibitions. (Early buying means placing large advance orders at the beginning of the season.)

TOYS "R" US IN JAPAN

This section will look into the Toys "R" Us strategy to adapt its formula to the Japanese market. The discussion is in five parts: Toys "R" Us expansion into Japan, store operations, pricing strategy, trade relationships, and penetration strategy.

Toys "R" Us Expansion into Japan

Toys "R" Us attracted attention when it opened its first store in December 1991 because it was the premiere large-scale retail enterprise by a foreign concern. As of August 1993, Toys "R" Us has opened seven stores and is scheduling 19 more. Targeting cities with populations exceeding 500,000 as trade areas, it plans to open 100 stores during the next decade.

Toys "R" Us has introduced its successful formula as the world's largest toy retailer: suburban location with plenty of parking space, self-service, everyday low prices, high volume, large-scale warehouse-style, and a vast selection of merchandise. This is known as the category killer store format. It has also brought along its key business practices to cut costs, dealing directly with manufacturers. All ingredients are new to Japan.

Store Operation

The stores are identical to the ones in the United States. Store size averages 4,100 sq. m. with selling space of about 3,000 sq. m. The locations are generally in suburbs with ample parking space for drivers' convenience. Five of seven stores have become anchor stores in community shopping centers.

Compared with the typical small Japanese shops that stock fewer than 3,000 items, and with specialty chains stocking about 5,000 items, Toys "R" Us offers vast selections of from 15,000 to 18,000 items. Toys "R" Us serves as a one-stop-shopping store for toys and other child-related merchandise.

Merchandising and inventory are controlled by the POS information system. Despite the huge number of items, inventory is optimized and maintained for efficient operations.

Among some 15,000 items, about 60% of the merchandise is domestic. Toys "R" Us plans eventually to raise the imports' proportion to 50%.

Pricing Strategy

Its discount pricing varies by item, generally ranging from 10% to 40%, or 50% at most, and always less than the manufacturer's suggested price. Toys "R" Us tactically offers a 30% discount for fast-moving domestic popular items and 50% for imported character goods.

It appears, however, that the discount rate is generally not so powerful as the 20% to 30% offered in the United States. Unlike in the United States where the company commands a quarter of the market, Toys "R" Us in Japan is still small. It is having a hard time winning low-cost, direct-supply contracts from Japanese toy manufacturers. It has thus encountered obstacles to its price-cutting strategy.

Trade Relationships

When Toys "R" Us started to negotiate with Japanese manufacturers, the basic concept of trade terms and conditions were: using its own distribution capability, quantity early buying, co-promotion, and co-advertising strategies. It pays the bill in cash after 90 days. Manufacturers ship their products to the Toys "R" Us distribution center and need not deliver to each store, except for some paper products. Toys "R" Us seemed to introduce several types of allowances to manufacturers. These allowances may make the deal complicated in a way, and Toys "R" Us could ask for greater discounts in the near future. Actually, Toys "R" Us, the revolutionary innovator challenging the Japanese distribution system, is now introducing new allowances relatively similar to those prevalent in local business practices.

Toys "R" Us is negotiating with using early buying practices. At this point, it is hard for the Japanese toy manufacturers to judge the prospects of Toys "R" Us. As stated earlier, the Japanese manufacturers have maintained strong relationships with wholesalers. They do not wish to upset their long-standing partners. For Toys "R" Us to gain direct deals, it requires a shift in the balance of power between retailers and manufacturers. Toys "R" Us has proved hard to replicate in Japan. So far, it claims to have signed up 50 Japanese toy manufacturers. But it has failed to persuade many others. Nintendo, the world's top video-game maker, has agreed to sell directly to Toys "R" Us, but at prices that will not offend wholesalers and other retailers. Nintendo sells its products through a group of about 70 wholesalers as well as through other middlemen.

Penetration Strategy

The initial obstacle to open outlets in Japan was to win approval under the Large-Scale Retail Store Law that regulates the opening of stores larger than 500 sq. m. It took Toys "R" Us three years of negotiations and legal process to open such a gigantic store because of the law. This law became the flashpoint in the wide-ranging trade talks known as the SII (Structural Impediment Initiative) between the United States and Japan. Abolishing or changing this law looked to be the symbol of the openness of the Japanese market and its distribution system to foreign companies. By April 1990, MITI agreed to shorten the large-store application process to no more than 18 months. The strategic decision of Toys "R" Us to penetrate the Japanese market was timely under the movement of modifying the Large-Scale Retail Store Law. Toys "R" Us was the first foreign firm to take advantage of the change.

Toys "R" Us successfully used the leverage of not only the political pressure to deregulate the law but also to press coverage to gain the attention of Japanese consumers. It told what Toys "R" Us was and how it had been successful as a discount store. Its opening day in Japan was the firm's most successful in history: the first single store drawing 17,000 customers. The second store opening was inaugurated by former President George Bush amid much fanfare. Consequently, consumers are impressed with Toys "R" Us as an innovative store format that provides a vast selection and strong discount pricing.

Another tactical success was in finding a strong local partner. This is McDonald's Corp. (Japan) headed by the well-known entrepreneur, Mr. Den Fujita. Under the terms of the joint venture, Toys "R" Us got help in its negotiations with the bureaucracy, in the selection of good sites, and in understanding Japanese consumers. The partnership has helped both companies. Most of the shopping centers being built by the local partners around Toys "R" Us will include a McDonald's as well as another American franchise Mr. Fujita controls in Japan: Blockbuster Video.

RESPONSE TO THE TOYS "R" US' ENTRY

There were various responses to the Toys "R" Us' entry into the Japanese market. These vary by the layer of the distribution, market positioning, strategy, etc. In this section, we focus upon the response from the Japanese toy industry, manufacturers, wholesalers, retailers/consumers as well as from foreign manufacturers.

Japanese Toy-Manufacturers' Response

Only one major Japanese toy manufacturer, Nintendo Co., which already has strong relations with Toys "R" Us in the United States, has publicly stated its willingness to deal directly with Toys "R" Us. Many other toy manufacturers are reluctant to do so because they can't ignore powerful wholesalers and long-standing loyal customers. Moreover, they are still looking at the progress of Toys "R" Us and seem to be awaiting structural changes in retailing to minimize the distortion. But we have already seen early movement that may show one direction. In response to Toys "R" Us, Bandai, the leading toy manufacturer, has reorganized its three affiliated wholesalers into a single sales company. Another major toy manufacturer, Takara, acquired its affiliated wholesalers as its wholesale division. Both movements are not only to reduce distribution costs but also to integrate the dealing function and to eliminate the objections to dealing with Toys "R" Us. The wholesale prices, however, charged by Bandai will not allow Toys "R" Us to discount so extensively. For Toys "R" Us, at least, this makes it possible to use its buying power by dealing with a single channel for one toy manufacturer. But these toy manufacturers' moves to improve distribution efficiency will influence the nation's wholesale structure as well as its retail.

There are some other effects apparent among Japanese manufacturers. Toys "R" Us's giant store has commodious space to display merchandise. Some smaller toy manufacturers that have difficulty in distributing their products are approaching Toys "R" Us to market their products. Consumers find some toys that are not commonly seen in other stores. Toys "R" Us in this way can provide opportunities to the smaller toy manufacturers and develop Japan's hidden toy market.

Other than toy manufacturers, Toys "R" Us deals with grocery manufacturers. Thus far their impressions of Toys "R" Us are relatively favorable. Toys "R" Us's order quantity is larger and they don't need to deliver the merchandise to each store through wholesalers but only to the distribution center, at infrequent intervals. These conditions are better than with Japanese supermarkets.

Foreign Toy Manufacturers

Toys "R" Us merchandise from overseas is now 40% of its offerings. It can provide foreign toy manufacturers with a new channel to bypass the complicated distribution system in Japan often cited as a barrier to trade. Some American manufacturers have already landed here to amplify their marketing in Japan. For example, 1991 was the fourth time for Mattel to establish a subsidiary in Japan. Hasbro, the world's largest toy manufacturer, acquired the Japanese wholesaler, Nomura Toy, in 1992. These foreign manufacturers' strategic changes seriously affect licensed manufacturers and wholesalers who had been marketing those products in Japan.

Retailers' and Consumers' Response

Toys "R" Us has brought price competition into Japan's toy market. Thus far the area is limited to where a Toys "R" Us is open. Consumers are impressed with the discounts that they have never before seen, especially of imported brands such as Lego and Fisher-Price. In areas where Toys "R" Us opened stores, GMSs such as Nagasakiya or Ito-Yokado and the specialty chain like Hello Mac or even independent shops sharply respond to discount their prices to meet the competition. But only those GMSs or chain stores that have strong financial resources can continue to pursue such low-pricing strategy.

For those who are weak, small retailers created The Japan Association of Specialty Toy Shops in September 1990. This organization aims to pool resources with other small toy retailers to buy large quantities at competitive prices. As of August 1993, some 380 stores have joined the association, and will start testing their cooperative buying targeting the Christmas and New Year season. In addition to purchasing collaboration, the association will study the rationalization and modernization of the distribution system.

The price competition among retail stores will spread as Toys "R" Us opens more stores. This will increase pressure upon wholesalers and manufacturers to cut costs and prices. In an ironic twist, some toy-store chains will be using this pressure to help them deal with suppliers at lower prices. If this competition continues, the retail structure will be greatly affected. It may put the traditional pricing and distribution system in serious trouble or even in danger of collapse.

Some consumers, especially the elderly, complain about Toys "R" Us. There is no staff to explain or advise the shopper. Whether Japanese consumers, regarded as the most finicky and pampered in the world, can really be satisfied by cut-rate service is a question (e.g., Tajima 1971, Yoshino 1971, and Czinkota and Lalonde 1984).

Recently, however, that value has begun to diminish to a large degree. This is proven by the declining sales in Japanese department stores. Consumers have become educated and are able to make judgments on the quality and prices of the merchandise and of the services provided. Consumers' sense of values has become more diversified. This has caused the market to become more fragmented according to their needs. There are many niche markets other than price. The influence of Toys "R" Us provides an opportunity for specialty retail outlets to differentiate and accommodate consumers' different needs. Some shops are already applying the niche marketing strategy. The deregulation of large-scale retail stores will open the way for the development of various types of stores. Accordingly, many different store formats will appear in the Japanese toy market.

Until now, Toys "R" Us seems successful in its entry because of its discount strategy as well as its locations. Providing plenty of parking slots, Toys "R" Us successfully meets the growing needs of Japan's auto-borne consumers. Seven of five Toys "R" Us outlets are anchor stores of shopping centers. Toys "R" Us has become a day-trip driving destination for families.

Inasmuch as Toys "R" Us has everything from diapers to bicycles, it can offer one-stop-shopping for households that have children of various ages. Toys "R" Us merchandising is well-designed to meet consumers' needs according to purchasing patterns.

Toys "R" Us provides a vast selection of merchandise that meets the diverse needs of today's selective Japanese consumers. Toys "R" Us claims that the market actually expanded because of the diverse product lines they introduced in European countries after one year of its entry.

But unlike the stores in those countries, some stores in Japan start to position trial toys for consumers' sampling.

Wholesalers' Response

As stated above, wholesalers face increasing pressure from retail competition. The retail structural change, such as the diminution of smaller independent retailers, will sharply affect the wholesale business. If other mass-retailing channels grow, wholesalers' financial function for retailers as well as the structure of multiple layers will no longer be necessary.

Wholesalers will be expected to play another important role in the distribution system. Some radical wholesalers are responding by restructuring their businesses. They plan to subcontract delivery functions to outside companies and to convert their businesses to value-added service companies specializing in merchandising and retailer-support. But this will require time, personnel, and investment. One solution for the smaller wholesalers might be a merger to realize economy of scale. Most wholesalers, however, are still trying to figure out what is going to happen in the toy-distribution business. They struggle to find an effective solution for their future course.

TRENDS IN JAPAN'S CHANGING TOY-DISTRIBUTION SYSTEM

Prior to the Toys "R" Us entry, the toy-distribution system had virtually no price competition. Japan has been a manufacturing and wholesaling-oriented market. The retail structure is fragmented. Nevertheless, small toy shops that have limited merchandise command an estimated 54% of total sales (Table 5). Wholesalers have thus played a larger role than merely supplying goods, and provide financial support for retailers. This is true even for toy-specializing chains that emerged in the mid-80s or GMS chain stores that utilized the wholesalers. Instead of eliminating intermediaries, chain stores have provided opportunities for wholesalers to proliferate. This also has helped small shops that are connected to wholesalers. The pricing structure, as stated earlier, is based on the distribution system and has enhanced it, and vice versa.

The competition among toy retailers was somewhat limited within the distribution system although the retail structure has been changing fast. Unincorporated mom-and-pop shops have been rapidly decreasing at an average annual rate of 4% in the last nine years (Table 6). They have been replaced by increasingly incorporated stores and by specialty chain stores at an annual pace of about 6% during the same period, as well as by GMS stores. Conversely, the number of wholesale establishments that sell toys has remained unchanged at about 4,600 during the same period.

Now Toys "R" Us has brought its formidable formula to Japan. Its everyday low-price strategy has introduced price competition into Japan. For now this price competition may not be as fierce as in other countries because of the difficulty in dealing directly with toy manufacturers. But Toys "R" Us has really shaken the toy-distribution system. Chain stores and GMSs have entered into price competition. Some other small retailers are establishing cooperative buying organizations to compete. These price-cutting movements that strive to win mass-quantity-buying merits appear

TABLE 6

Year \ Establishments	Total	Incorporated	Unincorporated	%	%
1968	9,842	1,047	8,795	10.6	89.4
1970	10,979	1,354	9,625	12.3	87.7
1972	12,753	1,717	11,036	13.5	86.5
1974	13,733	1,995	11,738	14.5	85.5
1976	16,044	2,493	13,551	15.5	84.5
1979	17,812	3,077	14,735	17.3	82.7
1982	16,605	3,431	13,174	20.7	79.3
1985	14,775	3,515	11,260	23.8	76.2
1988	14,335	4,333	10,002	30.2	69.8
1991	15,243	5,781	9,462	37.9	62.1

Source: Census of Commerce

to create a mass-retailing structure. As the price competition spreads that Toys "R" Us has brought, it will expedite retail structural change.

Another factor in toy retailing that Toys "R" Us triggered is a large-scale retail-store format. This has taken advantage of the deregulation of the Large-Scale Retail Store Law. The deregulation has opened the door for retailers to invent diverse store formats. Toys "R" Us as a large-scale outlet can carry a vast selection of merchandise to enable selective Japanese consumers to make optimal choices. Toys "R" Us provides a new store-format concept that satisfies consumers' needs: suburban locations with ample parking for drive-in consumers, and wide-variety merchandising for one-stop-shopping for households with children. Meeting such consumer needs, Toys "R" Us joined shopping-center developments in some locations. It increases efficiency in retailing and convenience for consumers. The success of Toys "R" Us in the toy and child-related market will assist retailers in other markets to develop new shop formats, applying the new entrant's concept.

As stated above, Toys "R" Us will expedite retail structural change and has provoked new concepts in retailing. These changes, however, will force a transformation onto the existing distribution system as a whole, which was based on a fragmented retail structure. As mass retailers grow, the power balance in the distribution system will shift to retailers as Toys "R" Us encouraged in other countries. Wholesalers must restructure their business to cope with the emergence of a mass-distribution system and price-cutting strategy. Secondary wholesalers will be eliminated along with the smaller shops. The wholesale function will require streamlining of the distribution system to cut costs. The pricing structure will change, as well. Prices will likely be determined by the actual cost bases of the channel, although business practices may take a relatively longer time to change. Other than distribution, wholesalers may play new roles, such as providing value-added retail-support services to various store formats. In such a new environment, manufacturers' strategy will change, also. Manufacturers' production will likely be based on retailers' order quantities, reflecting POS consumers' purchasing data. Some large retailers have already developed their own products (private brand) in cooperation with manufacturers. This will reduce risks and improve overall efficiency. As the retailers increasingly differentiate, consumers may be different according to channel. Manufacturers' marketing channel strategy will thus need careful evaluation considering each channel requirement.

As stated, the advent of Toys "R" Us has introduced fierce competition and will accelerate overall structural changes and power shifts in Japan's toy-distribution system.

REFERENCES

Czinkota, M. R. and Lalonde, B. J. (1984), "A Description and Analysis of the Japanese Distribution System for Consumer Products," National Center for Export-Import Studies, Georgetown University, Washington D. C., August.

Czinkota, M. R. (1985), "Distribution in Japan: Problems and Changes," Columbia Journal of World Business (Fall), 65-71.

Goldman, A. (1991), "Japan's Distribution System: Institutional Structure, Internal Political Economy, and Modernization," *Journal of Retailing, 67* (Summer), 154-183.

Kakeda, Y. (1992), "Ryutsu channel soshiki no henka to tenbo" (Revolution of Distribution Channel) *Japan Marketing Journal, 44,* 14-21.

Manifold, D. L. (1993), "Accessing Japan's Distribution Channels," in The Japanese Distribution System, Michael R. Czinkota and Masaaki Kotabe, ed. (Probus Publishing Company).

_____ and W. Lazer (1979), "Japanese Distribution Channels: Invisible Barriers to Market Entry," MSU Business Topics (Winter), 49-62.

Tajima, Y. (1971), "How Goods are Distributed in Japan," Tokyo: Walton Ridgeway & Company.

Yoshino, M. Y. (1971), "The Japanese Marketing System: Adaptations and Innovations," Cambridge, Mass. and London: The MIT Press.

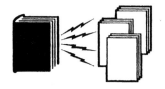

Haworth
DOCUMENT DELIVERY
SERVICE

This new service provides a single-article order form for any article from a Haworth journal.

- *Time Saving:* No running around from library to library to find a specific article.
- *Cost Effective:* All costs are kept down to a minimum.
- *Fast Delivery:* Choose from several options, including same-day FAX.
- *No Copyright Hassles:* You will be supplied by the original publisher.
- *Easy Payment:* Choose from several easy payment methods.

Open Accounts Welcome for ...
- Library Interlibrary Loan Departments
- Library Network/Consortia Wishing to Provide Single-Article Services
- Indexing/Abstracting Services with Single Article Provision Services
- Document Provision Brokers and Freelance Information Service Providers

---

MAIL or *FAX* THIS ENTIRE ORDER FORM TO:

Attn: **Marianne Arnold**
Haworth Document Delivery Service
The Haworth Press, Inc.
10 Alice Street
Binghamton, NY 13904-1580

or **FAX:** (607) 722-1424
or **CALL:** 1-800-3-HAWORTH
(1-800-342-9678; 9am-5pm EST)

PLEASE SEND ME PHOTOCOPIES OF THE FOLLOWING SINGLE ARTICLES:

1) Journal Title: _____

    Vol/Issue/Year: _____ Starting & Ending Pages: _____

Article Title: _____

_____

2) Journal Title: _____

    Vol/Issue/Year: _____ Starting & Ending Pages: _____

Article Title: _____

_____

3) Journal Title: _____

    Vol/Issue/Year: _____ Starting & Ending Pages: _____

Article Title: _____

_____

4) Journal Title: _____

    Vol/Issue/Year: _____ Starting & Ending Pages: _____

Article Title: _____

(See other side for Costs and Payment Information)

COSTS: Please figure your cost to order quality copies of an article.

1. Set-up charge per article: $8.00
   ($8.00 × number of separate articles) _____

2. Photocopying charge for each article:

   1-10 pages: $1.00 _____

   11-19 pages: $3.00 _____

   20-29 pages: $5.00 _____

   30+ pages: $2.00/10 pages _____

3. Flexicover (optional): $2.00/article _____

4. Postage & Handling: US: $1.00 for the first article/

   $.50 each additional article _____

   Federal Express: $25.00 _____

   Outside US: $2.00 for first article/

   $.50 each additional article _____

5. Same-day FAX service: $.35 per page _____

GRAND TOTAL: _____

METHOD OF PAYMENT: (please check one)

❑ Check enclosed   ❑ Please ship and bill. PO # _____
(sorry we can ship and bill to bookstores only! All others must pre-pay)

❑ Charge to my credit card: ❑ Visa; ❑ MasterCard; ❑ American Express;

Account Number: _____ Expiration date: _____

Signature: ✗ _____ Name: _____

Institution: _____ Address: _____

City: _____ State: _____ Zip: _____

Phone Number: _____ FAX Number: _____

MAIL or *FAX* THIS ENTIRE ORDER FORM TO:

Attn: **Marianne Arnold**
Haworth Document Delivery Service
The Haworth Press, Inc.
10 Alice Street
Binghamton, NY 13904-1580

or FAX: (607) 722-1424
or CALL: 1-800-3-HAWORTH
(1-800-342-9678; 9am-5pm EST)